THE PROFESSIONAL HOST

Cellar in the Sky. Courtesy of Windows on the World, World Trade Center, New York, NY.

THE PROFESSIONAL HOST

The Foodservice Editors of CBI

VNR Van Nostrand Reinhold
_____ New York

Library of Congress Catalog Card Number 80-15609

ISBN 0-8436-2154-0

Printed in the United States of America

Published by Van Nostrand Reinhold
115 Fifth Avenue
New York, New York 10003

Van Nostrand Reinhold International Company Limited
11 New Fetter Lane
London EC4P 4EE, England

Van Nostrand Reinhold
480 La Trobe Street
Melbourne, Victoria 3000, Australia

Macmillan of Canada
Division of Canada Publishing Corporation
164 Commander Boulevard
Agincourt, Ontario M1S 3C7, Canada

16 15 14 13 12 11 10 9 8 7

CONTENTS

PREFACE

Contemporary restaurant dining reflects the dramatic social changes that have taken place since the beginning of recorded history, especially within the last hundred years. Dining room designs have altered drastically in this century. They are destined to change even more rapidly in the centuries to come.

The American market has fallen in love with food and dining out. We in the foodservice industry must help and encourage our patrons to develop these feelings even further by presenting properly cooked, imaginative food in a well-styled manner. In response to an ever-changing and expanding world, restaurateurs are obliged to create sanctuaries not only to nourish the body, but to calm the soul as well.

We wrote this book because the increasing complexities of the foodservice industry demand a comprehensive text on dining room service for both students and professionals. Our research involved three years of study, in addition to endless conversations with our colleagues and other experts in the field. At this time we express our appreciation to those fellow professionals, too numerous to name here, whose expertise we consulted. For their invaluable support and assistance with research, we wish to thank all those who were involved in the development of this book. Their devotion and energy were essential to bringing *The Professional Host* to completion.

The result of their efforts and ours is an attempt to define, document, and explain what table service is in America. The opening chapters of *The Professional Host* provide you with the basic guidelines and information for becoming a qualified practitioner. The specific processes involved are then explained. Pictoral sequences are used to simplify these preparations and techniques. Lastly, we present control systems which may be used to maximize the productivity and profit of the operation. The emphasis throughout is on simplicity and precision, encouraging the student and professional to develop new and innovative service techniques that lend themselves to the overall refinement of the profession.

While the focus of this book is primarily a technical one, our commitment to the improvement of foodservice extends to the betterment of working conditions and the increase of opportunities for all. Many of the professional roles described herein have, until recently, been closed to women. However, we support the recent change of this phenomenon, and have used the words "waiter" and "he" only for simplicity's sake, in a general sense, to refer equally to women and men. It is our hope that this book will be a guide to all those interested in the continued development of gastronomy.

—*The Foodservice Editors of CBI*

THE PROFESSIONAL HOST

1
HISTORICAL PROFILE

The evolution of the foodservice industry began roughly 30 to 40 million years ago with the transmutation of ape to man. To share food, early human families either had to regurgitate the food consumed at the kill or slowly drag it back to the nest. Later, as humans evolved, they used their hands to carry food and threw rocks or swung clubs to acquire it. By 75,000 B.C. humans were skilled hunters. Indications of rites and rituals have been found dating from this period, implying an increased social consciousness.

Between 10,000 B.C. and 3,000 B.C. people began to turn from hunting and plant-gathering to domesticating livestock and cultivating plants. The first villages were established, and their people became less nomadic. Furthermore, they began to exercise more control over the availability of their food supply.

Up to this point in history, people had been preoccupied with obtaining food for survival. Simply stated, they ate to live. Once the food supply became more controllable, people started to live to eat. It was not long before custom, manners, etiquette, and regulations regarding food and its consumption were initiated. Before long society was dictating how, when, and with whom to eat; what and what not to eat; and even why to eat!

Of course there were concrete reasons for the development of certain customs. People were still at the mercy of climate, soil conditions, geographical location, and the overall abundance or lack of foodstuffs. But eating habits more and more began to be ruled by a feeling of propriety. From a means of survival, eating was evolving into an expression of identity.

ANCIENT EGYPT

Being a temperate and frugal people, the ancient Egyptians ate simply. They were rather hospitable and, unlike later, more restrictive cultures, the Egyptians permitted themselves to eat in the company of strangers, and men to eat in the company of women.

Caste differences in Egypt were most clearly reflected in dining room decor and furnishings. Peasants and artisans used simple pottery and sat on benches while eating in low mud houses. The airy palaces of the wealthy were surrounded by pools and gardens and were beautifully embellished with embroidered linens. Their furnishings included cushioned wooden arm chairs inlaid with gold and precious stones. The storage rooms were stocked with delicately carved wooden and ivory spoons, irridescent glass cups, and bowls of common gold, rarer silver, and the most valuable bronze.

ANCIENT GREECE

The Greek diet consisted of grains, milk, cheese, olives, and figs. Pigs and sheep served as a limited source of flesh. Greece exported olives and wine. From the fifth until the latter part of the first century B.C., the islands of Crete and Peloponnesos were the source of the finest wines in the Mediterranean world. Following the Egyptian custom, these sweet and heavily spiced wines were diluted with water.

The father of all Greek writers on cooking was Archestratus, who in the fourth century B.C. "diligently traversed all lands and seas in his desires ... of testing carefully the delights of the belly." His pronouncements of haute cuisine obscured the realities of everyday eating. While most Athenians had to tolerate salted or dried fish, Archestratus insisted that none but the fresh variety from Byzantium would do.

As the decades passed, tastes became more exotic. A pig that had died of overeating was a great delicacy. Geese were fed moistened grain to fatten them for the table. By the third century B.C., Athens had developed the first hors d'oeuvre trolley. Cooks prepared large trays with small plates containing garlic, sea urchins, sweet wine sop, cockles, and sturgeon.

CLASSICAL ROME

Wealthy Romans had highly sophisticated palates. The most costly and ostentatious table was proof of status. Elaborate presentations were in vogue: a hare decorated with wings to look like Pegasus (the winged horse of Greek mythology); a wild sow stuffed with lime thrushes; quinces stuck with thorns to resemble sea urchins. The range of ingredients available to Rome was remarkable. The wealthy imported pickles from Spain, ham from Gaul, wine from Jura, pomegranates from Lybia, oysters from Britain, and spices from Indonesia. Snails were bred and fattened on milk until they were too fat to retreat into their shells.

Upon arriving at a Roman banquet, guests were divested of their town clothing by slaves, and dressed in white robes and sandals. To ensure favorable auspices, guests took care to enter the banquet hall with the right foot. The number of guests seated at a single couch might be as low as three and as high as thirty, but was always a multiple of three — a number with divine significance. Napkins were used for the first time in Rome, each guest bringing his own. Spoons were still the only table utensil.

Most banquets were restricted to men; usually the only women admitted were dancing girls or courtesans. Emperor Augustus gave women official status in Roman society by inviting wives together with their husbands to banquets. Gossip at the table was common, and it became the custom for a host to place a rose on the table

as a sign that nothing said during the meal would be repeated afterwards. This led to the expression *subrosa*, which we still use today to mean "confidentially."

Extravagance prevailed. It became the custom at each important ceremony to serve a dish made with a hundred birds. Even this was not grand enough; a pie was made of the tongues of birds and only those that could sing or talk. Much wine was served. Each new wine was heralded with trumpets and the announcement of its name and vintage. There were up to twelve different wines served in the course of a single meal, domestic as well as imported. A connoisseur named Scarus boasted of having 195 different kinds of wine in his private cellar.

Many Roman emperors carried this extravagance to ridiculous, even vulgar, extremes. The Emperor Domitian once interrupted a debate in the Senate to ask which sauce should be served on the turbot at that night's banquet. Claudius was such a glutton that he had a slave tickle his throat with a feather to get rid of the excess and start anew. Marc Antony was so pleased with a banquet prepared for Cleopatra that he gave the cook a city.

Lucullus had files of menus listed according to cost — the more important the guest, the more costly the menu. Plutarch relates that one day Lucullus told his cook he was dining alone. The cook presented a simple dinner and was severely scolded. "But you were alone," protested the cook. Lucullus replied, "That's when you must take special pains. Today Lucullus is host to Lucullus."

Roman aristocracy tried to justify its excesses by the introduction of the *annoma*. This was the distribution of free grain by the authorities to relieve poverty. This institutional feeding of the poor was meant to induce calm among the masses, and to ease the consciences of government officials. The *annoma* eventually grew into a massive general subsidy which distorted both the economic and social structure of the state.

THE MEDIEVAL TABLE

Life in a feudal castle was difficult but exciting. The typical feudal dwelling was a tall narrow structure with one room to a floor. The ground floor was primarily a storeroom in which small animals were kept in the winter. The second floor was the living quarters, which served as a dining room, bedroom, and public hall. Most of the cooking was done in a separate kitchen in the courtyard, but sometimes meats would be roasted over a huge fire in the center of the second floor living space.

As there was no chimney, the smoke found its way out through a hole in the ceiling.

At meals the feudal lord and lady sat on a raised dais at one end of the room, while their retainers, children, and relatives settled on removable benches along the walls beside the open fire. When feasts were given, additional benches were brought into the big hall, relegating the retainers to eat in a separate room. The French word for bench is *banc*, hence the word "banquet." Many courses were served at feasts, with numerous dishes displayed on the table at the same time from which the diners made their selections. The table manners of the day dictated that two people drink from the same cup and eat from the same *tranchoir* or trencher. The trencher, made of hollowed stale bread, was seldom eaten and usually was thrown to the dogs or given to the poor. With no forks and few spoons available, the diners used fingers or short daggers to transport food from trencher to mouth. Bones and refuse were thrown to the floor, where eager dogs were always waiting for scraps. Rushes or grass mats were strewn thickly on the floor to absorb grease. By the end of a meal the floor was a paradise for scavengers. Eventually carpets were used in noble homes.

The scene at banquets must have been one of considerable activity. Most guests brought their own servants to stand behind their chairs to help serve and assist. There were always carvers for the meats, servants for the wines and numerous dishes, and tasters to ensure the noble lords that food and drink had not been poisoned. Dogs scavenged among the rushes while troubadours and acrobats entertained the guests during the intervals between courses.

AGE OF EXPLORATION

As Europe was broadening its influence around the world, gastronomy was exerting its influence on Europe. Shortly after the invention of moveable type printing in the fifteenth century, many works relating to food, wine, and the hygiene of gastronomy were circulated. Cookery as an art form resumed in Italy where it had once attained its highest level to date under Roman rule. French gastronomy in turn received impetus in 1533 when Italy's Catherine de Medici, accompanied by her entourage from Florence, arrived to become the queen of France's Henry II.

Possessing an abundance of superior wines, gifted with a natural aptitude for cookery, France soon strode ahead of Italy in the art of dining. The disparity can be seen in the reaction of the Venetian ambassador to

Paris in 1577. While the French culinary arts continued to improve throughout the reign of Henry III, the Venitian ambassador still could not bring himself to become enthusiastic about French food. He criticized the French for consuming too much meat and not enough bread, as well as for being gluttonous and eating four or five times a day.

The first public eating house in the western world, *La Tour d'Argent*, opened in Paris in 1533. Up to this time, the inns of England and France served travelers only *table d'hote* meals. At *La Tour d'Argent*, patrons could select from a whole series of exotic and unusual delicacies.

By the beginning of the seventeenth century, the French palate had grown still more sophisticated. A Frenchman had to possess some culinary acumen to be considered knowledgeable in the ways of the world. Louis XIII became his own cook, less for pleasure than for fear of being poisoned. Under the influence of Cardinal Richelieu, Louis' court developed a passionate interest in cookery. Kitchens were the center of attention, and it became fashionable for the host to prepare the main dish himself.

During the reigns of Louis XIV and Louis XV, it became stylish to "own" a famous chef. Great men stooped to simple trickery to win a rival's cook or steward; recipes were guarded like jewels. Diplomats and nobles were proud to lend their family name to a new sauce, Soubise and Bechamel being but two examples. France became fascinated by anything from the American colonies, not unlike the seduction of Americans today by anything French. Turkey stuffed with truffels became an instant hit.

It appeared that Napoleon and the French Revolution would abort France's culinary development, but this was not to be. True, the aristocrats were scattered, the servants demoralized, and the etiquette of court life erased; but the cooks of the fallen aristocrats needed employment. This proved to be a boom to the fledgling restaurant business. There was only one restaurant in Paris in 1765. By the end of the century there were five hundred.

One of the greatest chefs of this or any other era was Marie-Antoine Careme. He reduced the excessive repasts of the day to a more logical dinner by serving a proper progression of courses with an appropriate sequence of wines. However, Careme's most valuable contribution to the foodservice industry was his training of such disciples as Soyer and Fracatelli.

Auguste Escoffier, like Careme, was an innovator and organizer. He revamped the structure of the kitchen and defined the job of each worker. Escoffier was a prolific writer and a true scientist. Carefully observing the reactions of foods in the kitchen, he developed sound rules for food preparation and successfully communicated his expertise through his writings. Escoffier teamed up with the celebrated hostelier, Cesar Ritz, to open and operate many of Europe's finest hotels. With Escoffier in the back of the house and Ritz in the front, the level of public dining reached its zenith.

UNITED STATES

The eating habits of colonial United States did not escape Puritan influence. Eating was regarded as a momentary refueling to allow a body to return, recharged, to work. "Dining" was considered not only gluttonous but also slothful. The Puritan ethic that work was the most righteous human activity, combined with the pioneer ideology that to be particular about one's food was to be weak, established the mode of American fare — simple food unobtrusively presented.

While taverns, road houses, and even commercial operations had existed for sometime, the growth of the foodservice industry in the late 1700s and early 1800s centered around the hotel business. The United States was a vastly growing country. People travelled by stagecoach, canal boat, steamship, and railroad. While away from home, they needed a place to eat as well as to sleep. In the late 1700s, hotel food was usually served in a common room with no menu choice. By 1835, almost 300 visitors per day were looking for accommodations in New York City alone. Meals were served *table d'hote* without much ceremony, although the fare was substantial. As many as fifty or sixty dishes might be offered at once.

The American plan was the standard arrangement in the United States from the 1830s. Guests paid for meals and room together whether they wanted both or not. In 1855 the Parker House of Boston became the first American hotel to offer the European Plan, separating the concerns of bed and board, since the American Plan had become the standard.

"French" became synonymous with elegant dining in the 1830s. This simply meant that food was served on separate dishes instead of in the American fashion of putting everything on one plate. This French influence stemmed directly from our alliance with France during the Revolution as well as from the influx of French exiles into this country as a result of the reign of terror of Louis XVI. Brillat-Savarin, the famed author of *Physiologie de Gout*, was one of the French exiles who found

a home in the States. Fondues, ices, and bonbons were among the novel items introduced here by the French immigrants who also encouraged the increased consumption of soups, salads, sweet oils, and tomatoes. American idolatry of French eating customs still exists today.

Europeans in the early 1800s had mixed reactions to American cuisine. While the food itself was not criticized, the service was deplored. American foodservice establishments were admonished for seating everyone in a common room, offering little individual choice in the menu, serving too much food at one time, not pacing the meal, and rigidly fixing the eating hours for the convenience of management at the expense of the guest.

The American scene would change with the opening of Delmonico's in 1832. This New York restaurant set the standard for elegance in this country for the rest of the nineteenth century and is credited with teaching the American public how to enjoy fine dining. Delmonico's offered the first a la carte menu in New York City. European with an American influence, the menu offered a variety of indigenous fish and game as well as salads composed of New World plants. Yet Delmonico's success was not simply due to its good food but to the extras it offered, such as courteous service, private dining rooms, flowers, decorations, music, and fine wines and spirits. With the opening of Delmonico's, New York's foodservice industry began to flower. Within fifty years, there were between five and six thousand restaurants in New York City alone.

In New York, restaurant business received its impetus from the wealthy in business and industry; in San Francisco, restaurant growth sprang forth from mining wealth. In 1850 the population of California was only eight percent female. Miners had money but no one to fix their meals. Much of their cash was thus spent in the prospering restaurant industry. Other major cities such as Boston, Philadelphia, and New Orleans were also experiencing a growth in fine dining. As wealth spread across the country, so did food fashions. Throughout the nineteenth century, there was a marked increase in the national consumption of sugar, tea, coffee, fruits, and vegetables.

Chain restaurants and cafeterias were introduced in the late nineteenth century and had become quite popular by the beginning of the twentieth century. Cafeterias discovered that by letting patrons wait on themselves, costs could be lowered, menu prices dropped, and service speeded up. While many cafeterias were operated by women, they catered to businessmen.

Eating out was becoming more and more customary as restaurants and cafeterias increased in number. Restaurant expansion was largely due to the increased employment of women in business and the growth of apartment living. The United States was changing from an agrarian to an industrial society. With more people working away from home in plants, factories, and business, the restaurant lunch business accelerated. Besides cafeterias, a man could frequent a local tavern for lunch, while the working woman patronized the local drugstore that now served sodas and phosphates as well as sandwiches.

The wealthy could still find luxurious dining and service at hotel restaurants such as New York City's Waldorf-Astoria. Oscar Tschirky was the legendary maitre d'hotel at the Waldorf. "The art of dining," Oscar once said, "is certainly one of the half dozen outstanding contributions to man's rise from prehistoric to modern civilization." While working exclusively in the dining room, Oscar used his influence to cut down on the abundance of food served at a meal by simplifying the menu. As head of the dining room, he insisted that no staff member be allowed to have chin whiskers or a mustache, as he considered facial hair to be unsanitary. Oscar was also the first to install a plush rope behind which customers were made to wait until they could be seated. Under Oscar's artful direction, the Waldorf dining room was an integral part of the fabric of New York society.

Since the 1920s, foodservice in the United States has gone through many changes. The growth of the transportation industry has created a mobile society spending more time away from home. Railroad and airline feeding, fast-food operations, and the resort and tourist trades are but a few of the results of an attempt to feed our transient population. Industrial feeding and vending operations have evolved to provide food to the millions of workers who eat at least one meal per day away from home. In many ways, we are now back to the Puritan ethic of favoring simple food humbly served. However, as the speed of the twentieth century continues to accelerate, this choice stems more from expedience than from culinary preference.

Our melting pot society has had difficulty developing what might be called an American cuisine. With such a diverse populous, many ethnic styles of dining have emerged, each with economic variations. Italian, French, and Chinese restaurants that cater to lower-, middle-, and upper-class clientele can easily be found in many parts of the country. Yet as a nation of plenty trying to accommodate all people, we have created a rather homogenized cuisine.

With much of the population well fed, food has become a symbol of pleasure, security, power, and friendship. Food fads go in and out of style; restaurants become more specialized and stylized. What will the future bring? One thing is certain: the foodservice business has been on a continual upswing. More people are eating out than ever before. Some experts estimate that by the end of the twentieth century more than half the meals consumed in the United States will be away from home. It will take more professionally trained foodservice workers to meet this growing demand.

2
DINING ROOM ORGANIZATION AND PERSONNEL

The foodservice industry offers almost unlimited career opportunities to men and women. The rapidly expanding professions associated with "eating away from home" are rich in promise for the future. It is important for aspiring foodservice professionals to understand how people function together as a team. They should also be aware of the usual channels to follow for regular advancement within a particular firm and within the industry. For this, foodservice personnel can turn to the organization chart.

The organization chart is a management tool used to visualize chains of responsibility and authority. An understanding of this chain of command helps to establish teamwork and maximize the group's accomplishments. The organizational structure of each foodservice establishment will be unique to that establishment, but the goals are the same: customer satisfaction and financial success. The more the team of employees in an establishment can work together, the more productive their efforts at meeting these goals will be.

An example of a restaurant's organizational chart can be found in Figure 2.1. The amount of detail and the number of jobs listed in the chart are functions of the style and size of the operation. In most cases, the organizational chart will resemble a pyramid, with fewer people at the upper levels than at the lower ones. There is infinite possibility for variations in the organizational chart. The important thing to remember is that any given chart should reflect the real structure of the restaurant or business it represents, and the real interpersonal relationships and responsibilities therein.

In this example, the owner is ultimately responsible for the entire operation, and so is listed at the top of the pyramid. Immediately under the owner is the manager, followed by his or her assistant. This alignment indicates that the manager is fully responsible for those aspects of the operation as assigned by the owner. The assistant manager has broad responsibilities as delegated by the manager.

Below the level of assistant manager, we begin to see more specialized delegation of authority in the areas of the dining room and the kitchen. The fact that these areas are divided into two separate branches of the chart means that the person in charge of the kitchen, namely the chef, has no jurisdiction over the operation of the dining room. In another restaurant, the chef might have broader responsibilities, particularly if he is also the owner.

The organizational chart serves the vital role of informing people to whom they are directly responsible. It is a graphic representation of the chain of command. In our example, the busperson takes directions from the head waiter (or positions higher on this branch of the chart) but not from the chef, except when directed to do

6

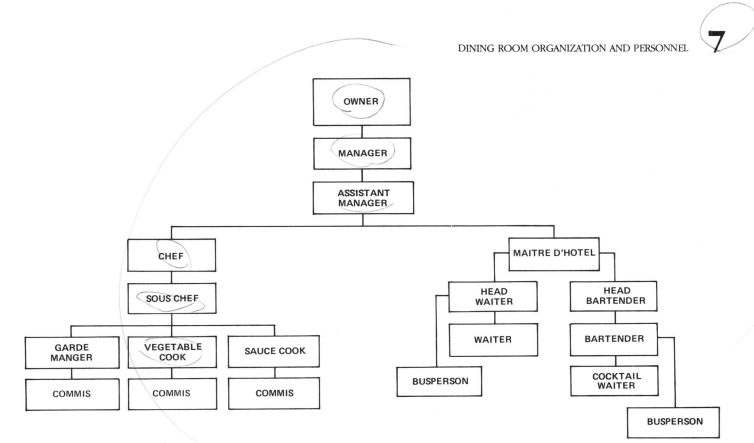

Figure 2.1. Organization Chart.

so by his or her superiors. In order to minimize friction in the working place, the owner or manager should avoid giving directions to this busperson, because these might conflict with what the head waiter has directed. The positions on the wide lower base of the pyramid should not be in the awkward situation of having to please two bosses nor should they be burdened with different sets of instructions for accomplishing the same task.

Besides defining the chain of command, the organizational chart also illustrates the possibilities for advancement within the firm. This helps employees to establish career goals and to understand what their next step upward might realistically be. For example, a busperson might aspire to become a waiter, then a head waiter, and later a maitre d'hotel.

JOB DESCRIPTIONS

A job description is a written summary of an individual worker's responsibilities and a description of the work to be performed. Most conventional job descriptions also include the relationship of the particular worker to others in the establishment and a list of the equipment to be used in performing the assigned tasks. Other items might also be included: the salary range of the position, amount of time allotted for each task, particular worker traits needed for the job, and experience and background necessary for the position.

Job descriptions are used differently depending on the needs of the organization. Some businesses will use the written job description in recruiting, hiring, placement, training, and evaluating their workers. Others will use it simply as a tool in organizational planning to see that all tasks are assigned with little or no overlap.

Employees gain from the use of good job descriptions. From job descriptions they know what is expected of them, to whom and for whom they are responsible, what they will be paid, the hours they will be expected to work and, overall, just what their jobs entail. In this way, no details are left to the whim of the supervisors, and the guests also benefit. A well-organized establishment, employing workers who know what they are doing, will be better able to provide efficient service to its guests.

MANAGEMENT STAFF

The management staff is responsible for the overall running of the operation. They must be knowledgeable and skilled in conducting business; handling money; hiring, training, and supervising employees; and monitoring the quality of food, beverage, and service. Depending on the size or type of operation, an employee might be responsible to one or more supervisors on the management staff, each of whom will have specific duties.

A list of the responsibilities of the manager would include the following:

Direct and supervise all activities pertaining to employee relations, food production, sanitation, guest service, and operating profits.

Promote good employee and public relations.

Coordinate production and service programs as directed by and in accordance with company policy and standards.

Observe all personnel for adherence to job descriptions, personal appearance, and efficiency; and, when necessary, make replacements.

Confer with kitchen personnel and coordinate purchasing requirements and receiving procedures.

Order supplies, serviceware, equipment, maintenance, and repairs.

Prepare, maintain, file, and submit reports, including employee time and personnel records.

Report employee grievances.

Maintain proper procedures in ordering, receiving, and storing foods, beverages, and supplies.

Be responsible for cash register procedures, including readings, cash drawers, register tapes, bank deposits, guest–check analysis, and report forms.

Act as the host when necessary.

Be responsible for restaurant and food sanitation, employee hygiene, and legal considerations such as public and employee safety.

An assistant manager would be responsible for assuming those responsibilities listed above that have been delegated by the manager.

KITCHEN STAFF — BACK OF THE HOUSE

The work of the kitchen staff is vital to the success of a foodservice unit. The preparation of food must be organized and scheduled for ease of operation. There must be standards of quality, style, and quantity for all items served. This can easily be accomplished by dividing the kitchen work into three steps:

1. Pre-preparation: preparing raw foods for cooking
2. Preparation: combining prepared foods according to standard recipes
3. Finishing: serving the completed product

Customers want consistency in the quality of the food they are served. On repeat visits, they want their orders prepared in the same manner, and served in the same quantity.

From an operational standpoint, uniformity of food preparation is imperative to efficient, smooth performance. Failure to adhere to portion standards raises food costs, undermines the profit structure, and makes proper inventory control virtually impossible to maintain. It is essential, therefore, that a set of food preparation and service standards be given to the new cook as part of the job manual. Standard recipes may also be included.

DINING ROOM STAFF — FRONT OF THE HOUSE

The dining room staff are the sales and service personnel; their functions include all activities concerned with customer relations. They sell and serve the food and beverage while controlling the sales by accounting for them in a prescribed manner.

The dining room staff is responsible in three primary areas:

1. Reception: taking reservation; greeting, aiding, and guiding the guests; presenting the menu
2. Sales: requesting orders; helping with selection; serving; answering questions; supplying other services; presenting the check
3. Sales control: checking food for quality and quantity; writing the check; serving as cashier

Service is the most important ingredient to the success of a restaurant, for even fine food cannot compensate for lack of detail in the dining room. Proper service to every customer depends on the actions of all employees throughout the day. No matter how tired or pressed for time a service person is, he must be pleasant and efficient for customer satisfaction.

The actual duties of a given station of the dining room will be defined by the style of restaurant and the type of service dictated by the management. Some restaurants and hotels will employ a maitre d'hotel, head waiter, captains, waiters, and buspersons. Other establishments will find that a host and a number of waiters are sufficient. Flexibility is the key – adapt to the system that is being used at your particular operation.

Maitre d'Hotel (Host or Hostess)

A competent maitre d', host, or hostess, is a substantial asset to the operation. Customers often decide to patronize a restaurant because of the recognition, greeting, and degree of care extended by the maitre d'.

Often the maitre d'hotel is in complete charge of the dining room operation, including duties at times left to the food and beverage manager. The maitre d'hotel may be responsible for the hiring, training, and firing of all dining room staff, and for setting up work schedules and assignments. (If a head waiter is employed, these duties may fall under his authority.) The maitre d'hotel might also:

Welcome guests. The average diner enjoys being greeted when entering. This establishes the mood for courteous and attentive service.

Aid guests with parcels or wraps.

Select a suitable table and guide guests.

Assist in seating and, sometimes, take an order to be passed to a station waiter.

Enter bookings and reservations in the reservation book.

Assist in resetting the table after guests leave.

Be responsible for cash accounting, banking procedures, and point of sale information.

Oversee maintenance of a clean and orderly dining room.

The guest who must wait for a table should not be made to feel forgotten. Unattended patrons may consider this an affront to their sense of dignity and importance. The host or hostess should attempt to mitigate this unpleasant situation by communicating often with the waiting guests.

Captain (Head Waiter or Head Waitress)

Some organizational systems differentiate between the head waiter and the captain, the head waiter taking charge of the entire dining room and the captain functioning as a section manager. Under some systems neither the head waiter nor the captain actually serves the guests; this is left to the waiter. As part of his or her responsibilities, the captain might also:

Assist the host in guiding guests to tables and seating them.

Warmly greet guests at table.

Suggest cocktails, aperitifs, and house specialty items; being knowledgeable about ingredients, garniture, and available name brands.

Take orders for beverages (in proper rotation to facilitate delivery), using standard abbreviations.

Present the menu.

Assist with the menu selection, selling menu items and being knowledgeable about preparation time, cooking technique, and possible delays.

Take food orders in proper rotation, using standard abbreviations.

Be knowledgeable about tipping procedures.

Know and practice proper sanitation procedures in dining room, service areas, and kitchen.

Know and practice safety, accident, and fire prevention rules.

Be adept with solid and liquid alcohol fuels for tableside preparation.

Possess information useful to guests about the restaurant's services, local tourist attractions, and night spots.

Learn the names of regular customers and their preferences for foods, beverages, and table assignments; know names and titles of local VIPs as well as department heads in the establishment.

Handle customer complaints and problems amicably.

Know the names and uses of all equipment and utensils that dining room personnel use in carrying out dining room du'

Know dining room lingo.

Assume responsibility for iss' station.

Assign waiter stations, tal rotation schedule.

Inspect dining room ness, repair, ar

Waiter or Waitress

The particular responsibilities of waiters and waitresses will depend on such factors as style of service, type of restaurant, and volume of business. Generally, a waiter or waitress is expected to:

Arrange, set up, and serve guest tables.

Set up and clean service equipment and assigned stations.

Keep tables and serving areas stocked, cleaned, and in good repair.

Have working knowledge of all food and beverage items offered on menu, including basic kitchen techniques, tableside food preparation, proper garniture, ingredients, and pronunciation of all menu items.

Know and use correct serving techniques for all types of food and beverage offered on the menu.

Know and practice principles of food sanitation, fire prevention, safety, accident prevention, personal health, and cleanliness. Know and adhere to house rules and regulations.

Deal with emergencies quickly and efficiently.

Practice good customer relations through knowledge of establishment, facilities, and personnel.

Have knowledge of the local area and related information.

Handle guests' belongings.

Deal with problems and complaints courteously and efficiently.

Service Attendant and Other Personnel

The responsibilities of a service attendant, or bus-person, will vary as much as those of a waiter. Generally the service attendant will be called upon to:

Assist the station waiter.

Bring food checks to kitchen.

Transport dishes and trays to side tables.

Remove plates from guest tables.

Return used dishes, glassware, and flatware to service area or kitchen.

A number of other service personnel are needed to complete the professional foodservice staff.

entice.   Apprentices progress upward through osts. In continental brigades, young waiters *iccolos*, or little ones.

Server and Passer (Trolley Assistant Waiter). The server is generally an assistant waiter who is assigned to an hors d'oeuvre trolley, pastry cart, hot box for fresh rolls, or similar station.

Wine Waiter (Wine Butler).   In many operations, the tasks of the wine waiter are performed by the head waiter, captain, or waiter. Conventionally, the wine waiter would:

Present the wine list.

Suggest a wine.

Assist with the wine selection.

Establish the quantity for needs of the table.

Take the wine order.

With requested input from guest, determine the desired service time of the wine.

Know correct serving temperatures of wine and assure that wines are served at appropriate temperatures.

Present the bottle.

Open the wine and present the cork to the host.

Pour the first ounce and offer it to the host for approval.

Know and practice decanting procedures.

Serve wine in proper order.

Replace unacceptable wine.

Carver (Trancheur).   This position is rarely found in today's restaurants. The nineteenth-century writer Vatel wrote of the Trancheur:

"Pleasing, civil, amicable, and well-disposed, he should present himself at table with his sword at his side, his mantle on his shoulder, and his napkin on his left arm...grave and dignified, his appearance cheerful, his eyes serene, his head erect and well combed, abstaining as much as possible from sneezing, yawning, or twisting his mouth, speaking very little and directly, without being too near or too far from the table."

This is good advice for all dining room positions today.

Restaurant Personnel for French Service

The line of authority in French service is somewhat more detailed than in American service. Whereas more personnel are involved, each station has specifically defined duties and tasks.

Maitre d'Hotel: The Maitre d' is solely and completely in charge of the entire dining room operation.

Chef de Salle: Similar to head waiter of American service, the Chef de Salle is in charge of the actual running of the dining room and supervises all dining room staff.

Chef de Rang: The captain or section manager, the Chef de Rang takes all orders in a particular section, prepares all tableside items in the section, plates all food in the section, and supervises staff in the section.

Demi-Chef de Rang: Acting as a backwaiter, the Demi-Chef de Rang picks up food from kitchen and sets up the gueridon with the *mis en place*.

Commis de Rang: The front waiter, the Commis de Rang serves meals from gueridon to the table and sets the silver prior to each course.

Commis de Suite: The Commis de Suite apprentices the back waiter.

Commis Debarrasseur: Acting as apprentice to the front waiter, the Commis Debarrasseur clears the table.

PERSONAL CHARACTERISTICS OF THE PROFESSIONAL HOST

The characteristics of the successful professional host can be divided into two major categories — physical (professional appearance and personal hygiene) and behavioral (personality traits of the professional host). The comments that follow should serve as guidelines for aspiring front-of-the-house personnel.

As a professional host, you must remember that the first and possibly most lasting impression you make on a person is through your appearance. Make it a positive one. Good grooming is a must for anyone working in the front of the house. The uniform one wears to work, be it a waitress' dress, a tuxedo, or a stylized costume, is a badge of professionalism and should be worn with pride. Moreover, the well-groomed person always looks and is clean. Clothing should fit properly; shoes should be shined and in good condition, including the heels. For more information, read the sections on personal hygiene and career apparel in chapter 3, and apply the principles to your everyday grooming habits.

Perhaps the other most important trait you can possess as a truly professional front-of-the-house personnel is the ability to deal with people. No amount of polish or knowledge can replace the element of caring for the customers' happiness. This most humanistic of personal traits does not always come easily. We are all familiar with the cranky, demanding restaurant customer, who aggravates service personnel while expecting them to be pleasant and efficient in return. We all have bad days occasionally, but the professional host never lets this become apparent to the guests.

In addition to being adept with the public, a person in the front of the house must have characteristics possessed by any individual of integrity, particularly as it relates to the conduct of business. Following are listed some of the many traits desirable for those working as professionals in the service of foods and beverages.

Attentiveness. The professional host is not a daydreamer, nor is he absentminded. He must be constantly alert to the needs of the guests, who should never have to work to attract a service person's attention. The station must never be left unattended. The power to perceive what is happening, and what is about to happen, calls for more talent than most realize. The professional host must have an ongoing knowledge of what is transpiring at each of the tables. It is necessary to keep a discreet watch on the diners' progress through their meal. Anticipating when more wine should be poured, when the table will need to be cleared, or how orders should be coordinated requires that one's attention is riveted to the job at hand.

Courteousness. Besides being available to deal with requests, it is important to assist in those areas that relate to the customer's comfort. This includes such tasks as helping guests with chairs, packages, coats, and dropped items; lighting cigarettes and changing ashtrays; correcting glare from lights or the sun; eliminating drafts; and adjusting the sound level of music if necessary. The magic words, "please," "thank you," and "excuse me" are essential in the vocabulary of food-service personnel. Polite words and considerate actions indicate a regard for others — for fellow employees and guests alike.

Dependability. Dependability is really a sign of maturity and is a desirable trait for individuals in any profession. The dependable person can be relied on to accomplish what he promises, to be at work during agreed upon hours, and to fulfill commitments. Dependability is a major factor employers consider in hiring.

Economy. Professionals in any business are responsible for doing their share to keep costs down. Untold amounts of revenue disappear daily in foodservice establishments through waste — the largest and most uncalled-for expense in the industry. Common sense is an important key to economy in the foodservice industry. A rational person does not deliberately destroy or dispose of personal or business property. The professional host avoids waste by:

Careful handling and stacking of china and glassware

Taking pains not to discard silverware with refuse

Avoiding unnecessary soilage of linen

Serving standard-sized portions

Returning unused items to the kitchen whenever possible and legal

Asking the guest before replenishing butter, rolls, and coffee

Using the proper amount of cleaning preparations; (misuse can damage the item being cleaned)

Efficiency.   Acting efficiently means doing less work with better results. The ability to catalog orders and plan trips to the kitchen and service area saves steps. The time saved by being organized can be spent on better serving the customer.

Honesty.   Honesty is an important trait for anyone, particularly an individual who is dealing with the public. During the course of a regular business day any member of the dining room staff has innumerable opportunities to deceive both the restaurant and the guest. Consequently, the professional host must be above reproach in all aspects of his day-to-day routine.

Knowledge.   The professional host must be equipped to respond to any number of questions that customers may ask. He must be able to work through busy periods without continually making inquiries of fellow employees. It is imperative, therefore, to take the time to know the menu and locate the equipment in the dining room well before this information is actually needed. An awareness of the physical features of the dining room and kitchen can help the server to speedily solve any problems that arise. In addition, it is necessary to know the ingredients of all menu items, their preparation time, their proper service temperature and garnishes.

The professional host's knowledge of the establishment's special services, hours of operation, and special facilities is good for business, and can be a real help to new customers. Community news, future and current events, and local places of interest are all topics on which the professional host should be informed.

By reading books on wines and foods, the professional host appears more knowledgeable in discussions with the guest and learns to appreciate the complexities of the culinary field. Winning the confidence of guests by being knowledgeable will generate goodwill and increase tips. The successful professional host takes the time on and off of the job to work at being well-informed.

Loyalty.   The professional host endeavors to obey regulations and behave positively toward the firm for which he is working. Loyalty is also demonstrated by maintaining quality standards.

Preparedness.   The foodservice hospitality industry is not a business for procrastinators. It makes the utmost sense to always think and work ahead. Have everything ready before service begins: putting off work that can be done in advance, such as stocking side stands and folding napkins, usually means having to do it later when time should be spent on the customer. Having proper equipment (a corkscrew, matches or a lighter, an extra pencil or pen) also helps to make service personnel appear more professional in the eyes of the guest.

Productivity.   While grace and showmanship contribute to the making of a successful front-of-the-house staff member, the ability to get the job done is no less important. The best combination of these traits is a balanced one. One should enjoy performing, particularly if employed at doing tableside cookery. At the same time, a person must be a real worker — one who always remembers that excellent service for the guests is the first goal.

Quietness.   The front of the house is not a place for employees to be chatty. Service personnel should speak only concerning business, so limit talking with fellow workers to the job at hand. Unless the customer initiates a conversation, the only subject of discussion with guests should be the service of the meal. Speak in a clear voice with pleasant intonation, and never be loud. Good service is silent.

Sensitivity.   To many guests, particularly at breakfast or lunch, a meal is only an interruption in a series of other events, and not an end in itself. Even the devoted gastronome occasionally has a train to catch or a theatre engagement scheduled immediately after mealtime. It is important to be sensitive to the guest's desire for quick service in these cases. While the customer should never be rushed, the professional host can expedite the meal in pleasant ways, such as suggesting menu items with minimal preparation times, which enable speedy service.

Skill. In order to advance in his career, the professional host must be willing to work constantly at upgrading his skills. Acquiring a skill is the development of proficiency in an art or craft. The way to improve skills is by practice. The ability to move through crowds and precision at tasks such as tableside carving are examples of skills acquired with practice.

Tact. The ability to say or do the right thing at the right time without offense to others is important for anyone dealing with the public. The professional host takes care in correcting a misinformed guest and always steers the conversation into safe, agreeable channels.

Persuasiveness. Even before the actual service of the meal begins, the professional host must "sell" the guest on what to order. Selling increases the check average. This, in turn, increases the restaurant's profits, and the gratuities as well. Subtly, a good waiter will steer guests away from choosing certain menu items and induce them to order others. As the guests enter the dining room, the professional host should determine whether to try selling them expensive items or extras, or whether to suggest items that are more of a bargain. It helps to be able to sense whether the guests are likely to want a simply prepared, standard dish, or a more elaborate and unusual one. If done properly, selling will magnify the satisfaction that the customer derives from the dining experience.

3
SAFETY AND SANITATION

Whenever a service function is performed a concerted effort should always be made to assure the personal safety of everyone in the facility — guests and fellow workers alike. Accidents do not just happen. They are caused by neglect, carelessness, thoughtlessness, and ignorance.

THE SEVEN COMMANDMENTS OF SAFETY

Listed are seven general rules of safety. Learn them and follow them at all times:

1. Safety is everyone's business. Consider yourself a member of the safety committee. Report unsafe conditions immediately.
2. When you see anything on the floor that does not belong there, be it a spill or an object, remove it.
3. Report all injuries no matter how slight, and get immediate first aid.
4. Walk, do not run, especially in halls or on stairs. Always keep to the right and be particularly watchful at corridor intersections.
5. Be especially careful with swinging doors. If there is a window panel, look before

opening; if not, open the door slowly, using the handle or push plate.
6. Avoid horseplay and practical jokes. Harmless fun can result in injury.
7. Report all defective equipment and obey safety rules when you are working with any equipment.

Falls account for the largest percentage of accidents in foodservice operations. Some common causes are:

Objects in corridor or on stairs

Equipment and electrical cords in passageways

Dirt, trash, or other items left on floors

Wet or oily floors, spills that have not been wiped up

Unsafe ladders, chairs, and window sills (A ladder should be tall enough for you to do your job comfortably when standing at least one step from the top.)

Chairs being left in traffic aisles in the dining room

People can easily fall over furniture, cords, and equipment. For this reason, no apparatus should be left in paths of traffic. Never leave anything in stairwells or near doors. To avoid tripping, keep cords off of the floor. Furniture or equipment must be put back where it belongs as soon as you finish using it. Falls on stairs may be caused by a loose tread or other faulty part of the stair or railing. Report any such disrepair at once. Be sure to keep chairs out of dining room traffic aisles.

BODY MECHANICS

Every time you move you use body muscles. In table service, tasks are required that use many muscles at one time. Constant and repeated use of muscles can cause tiring and fatigue. Once tired, you are more prone to accidents. Proper weight distribution and posture can eliminate fatigue.

Incorrect movement of the body or the use of infrequently used muscles can cause strains and sprains. These types of injuries often result from improper lifting and moving of objects, mistaking one's strength, carelessness, and poor use of arms and legs. The occurrence of strains and sprains can be lessened by the use of smooth motions and by keeping the body in balance.

Using several movements of the body together correctly is known as *body mechanics*. This includes posture and the use of the body in moving, lifting, carrying, pushing, and pulling objects. Understanding the principles of body mechanics will help reduce accidents.

Posture. Posture is the way the parts of the body are lined up. Weight must be balanced correctly with the spine as the central line for standing, sitting, and walking. Good posture allows you to work smoothly, with the least amount of strain. It also improves general appearance.

Standing. The proper way to stand is with the head erect, eyes facing directly ahead, chest up and forward, stomach pulled in, and feet naturally placed to balance body weight. Proper standing aids breathing and improves circulation. This results in reduced fatigue.

Muscle use. When performing any task, use the greatest number of muscles and muscle groups possible. Use two hands rather than one. This will make the workload less tiring.

Leg and arm muscles. The leg and arm muscles are stronger than back muscles. When lifting heavy objects use leg and arm muscles as much as possible to take the load off of the back and other muscles that are relatively weak. Rather than bending from the waist, kneel or squat when performing a task near the floor. This reduces tiring and straining of the back muscles.

Direction of movement. Develop rhythm and go with the movement of the task at hand. Avoid twisting as much as possible, particularly when lifting heavy trays.

Lifting. Never lift a heavy object alone. If an object is too heavy to lift, you should do one of the following:

Ask for assistance.
Divide the load and make several trips.
Push, drag, or roll it.
Have someone stronger lift it.

To lift an object from the ground or a low position:

1. Stand near the object with your feet slightly apart.
2. Stoop close to the object by bending your knees.
3. Keeping the back straight, take hold of the object firmly.
4. Lift the object by pushing up with the leg muscles.
5. Keeping the load close to the body, rise to a standing position.
6. Upon rising, move one foot diagonally back from the other.

Carrying. Never carry an object that will obstruct your view. To carry an object:

1. Keep your back as straight as possible.
2. Keep the weight load close to the body and centered over the hips.
3. Lean back slightly to counterbalance the weight of the load.
4. Divide the weight between both hands.
5. Put the load down by bending at the hips and knees. Keep the load close to the body; do not reach.

Pushing and pulling motions. Use arm and leg muscles, never back muscles, when pushing and pulling. To push an object:

1. Stand close to the object to be moved.
2. Stoop or crouch if object is low. Keep feet apart.
3. Bend the elbows and put hands on object at chest level.
4. Lean forward, keep back straight, and push with arm and leg muscles.

To pull an object:

1. Place the feet apart, one foot in back of the other, keeping close to the object.
2. Grasp firmly, crouching and leaning away from the object.
3. Pull the object by straightening your legs, keeping the back straight.
4. Walk backwards with bent knees.

Motion economy. Motion economy eliminates unnecessary waste of time and energy. Improving work methods will result in less fatigue. The following tips should always be kept in mind:

Motions should be productive and organized. There is unnecessary movement in searching for materials and tools. There should be an orderly place for them.

Motions should be simple. Use only motions needed to perform the task.

Motions should be rhythmic. Smooth motions are less tiring and actually less work.

Equipment should be within easy reach.

Tools and materials should be in a definite position.

Be at ease. Good posture and proper use of muscles and parts of the body help you to relax.

FIRE SAFETY

Fires present two clear dangers: the injury and destruction caused by the actual fire, and the panic and fear that overcome people and hinder them from thinking and acting rationally. Practicing fire safety encompasses both preventing fires and doing the right thing if a fire breaks out.

The best way to fight fire is to prevent fire. Like accident prevention, fire prevention depends on the common sense of everyone working in the operation. Service personnel must be sure to follow these measures:

See that ashtrays and receptacles are provided and used in all areas of the dining room.

Take care in cleaning ashtrays. Never empty them directly into waste baskets or other rubbish containers.

Never use a defective electrical outlet.

Never use an improper extension cord or adapter.

Never overload a circuit.

Report all frayed cords and loose connections.

Take special care when lighting gas jets or alcohol burners on a gueridon.

Extinguish all flames before moving gueridon in the dining room.

Exercise extreme caution when flambeing food in the dining room.

If a fire does break out, the emergency action taken in the first five minutes is extremely important. To be prepared in the event of a fire, know the floor plan of your area and the entire building, be familiar with exit routes and alternatives, and know the exact location of fire extinguishers and how to use them. Here is how to help fight a fire once it has started:

1. Do not panic.
2. Assist guests to safety.
3. Pull nearest fire alarm box.
4. Notify main switchboard and fire company as to the exact location and nature of the fire.
5. Send someone to direct the firemen when they arrive.

Fires and Other Emergencies

Fires are categorized into four classes:

Class A: fires of ordinary combustible materials such as wood, cloth, paper, and many forms of plastic — anything that burns and leaves an ash residue

Class B: flaming gases and liquids of appreciable depth such as fat, oil, grease, and paint

Class C: electrical fires

Class D: combustible metals

Know the types of fire extinguishers kept by the restaurant in which you work; use them only in cases of fires for which they were intended. To put out a class A fire, a water solution or multipurpose dry chemical extinguisher is most effective.

Class B fires are best extinguished with some type of carbon dioxide or chemical powder such as sodium bicarbonate or potassium bicarbonate. These types of extinguishers will smother the fire, depriving it of oxygen. Foam extinguishers can be used with some, but not all, types of liquid fires. Check the extinguisher label for restrictions. Restaurants are particularly susceptible to grease and fat fires. Do not use water on such a fire. Not only will water fail to extinguish the fire, but it may cause the grease or oil to overflow and therefore spread the fire.

Class C fires should be smothered with an inert gas or dry chemical extinguisher. Because water conducts electricity, never use it to extinguish an electrical fire. Class D fires, which are highly unlikely in restaurants, are best extinguished with some form of dry-compound extinguisher.

Burns

Some dining room equipment and utensils can cause severe burns. Always move or position hot plates and platters with the aid of a side towel. Verbally inform guests and other service staff whenever any serviceware is hot. Leave a side towel draped over the cover or at the edge of any hot receptacle. Hot beverages are another potential hazard. Remember, service should never be rushed: take care in transporting hot liquids, especially when moving through a crowded dining room. All serious burn injuries should receive medical treatment immediately.

Choking

Food choking is one of the leading causes of accidental death. Unless treated, a choking victim will die in four minutes. The choking victim may exhibit some of these symptoms:

Panic
Inability to breathe
Inability to speak
Blue skin
Collapse

The Heimlich maneuver is generally considered the best first aid for choking. Caution is recommended however. Any administrator of first aid must, according to law, exercise "reasonable care and skill" or else be liable for negligence. (See Figure 3.1, p. 18.)

Emergency Procedures

In the event of any kind of accident or emergency, each foodservice establishment will have its own specific course of action. Here are some general guidelines to follow whenever an emergency occurs:

Do not panic.
Call or send for help immediately and give explicit details as to the location and nature of the accident.

Do what needs to be done in a logical order.
When giving first aid, do not attempt more than you are qualified to do.
Things are expendable, people are not. Do not endanger yourself or anyone else.
As there is seldom time to consult a book when faced with an emergency, be aware beforehand of what to do and how to do it.
Write a report covering the details, location, and severity of the accident as soon as the emergency has been taken care of.

SANITATION AND HYGIENE

No matter how well-designed the foodservice operation, the impression instantly conveyed by such things as a stained cloth, fingered cutlery, soiled glass, or an unsightly employee will undermine the confidence in the operation. In addition, unsound sanitary practices can threaten the health and well-being of the patrons and workers of an establishment. Consequently, strict observance of the following rules is essential.

Have physical and dental examinations at least once a year.
Take a bath or shower daily.
Use a deodorant.
Keep hair clean, neat, and under control.
Wear clean, suitable clothes at all times.
Keep lockers neat and clean.
Eat a balanced diet of wholesome food.
Wash your hands well with germicidal dispenser soap and hot water before starting work, after using the toilet, after smoking, and before preparing food.
Wear a clean apron or uniform and a hair net or cap.
Do not wear jewelry or hair ornaments that may drop into food.
Keep fingernails clean and never wear polish.
Always keep a clean rubberized bandage on any cut or sore. Rubberized finger cots are particularly effective in guarding finger cuts.
Keep your hands away from your scalp, face, arms, and eyes.
Never use a side towel to wipe your face or arms.
To prevent pencils and pens from falling into food when you bend over, keep them in pockets below the waist. Of course, never put them in your mouth or behind your ear.

A person choking on food will die in 4 minutes – you can save a life using the HEIMLICH MANEUVER*

Food-choking is caused by a piece of food lodging in the throat creating a blockage of the airway, making it impossible for the victim to breathe or speak. The victim will die of strangulation in four minutes if you do not act to save him.

Using the Heimlich Maneuver* (described in the accompanying diagrams); you exert pressure that forces the diaphragm upward, compresses the air in the lungs, and expels the object blocking the breathing passage.

The victim should see a physician immediately after the rescue. Performing the Maneuver* could result in injury to the victim. However, he will survive only if his airway is quickly cleared.

If no help is at hand, victims should attempt to perform the Heimlich Maneuver* on themselves by pressing their own fist upward into the abdomen as described.

WHAT TO LOOK FOR

The victim of food-choking:

1. Can Not Speak or Breathe.

2. Turns Blue.

Heimlich Sign: Hand to neck signals: "I am choking!"

3. Collapses.

HEIMLICH MANEUVER*

RESCUER STANDING
Victim standing or sitting

☐ Stand behind the victim and wrap your arms around his waist.

☐ Place your fist thumb side against the victim's abdomen, slightly above the navel and below the rib cage.

☐ Grasp your fist with your other hand and press into the victim's abdomen with a **quick upward thrust.**

☐ Repeat several times if necessary.

When the victim is sitting, the rescuer stands behind the victim's chair and performs the maneuver in the same manner.

OR

RESCUER KNEELING
Victim lying face up

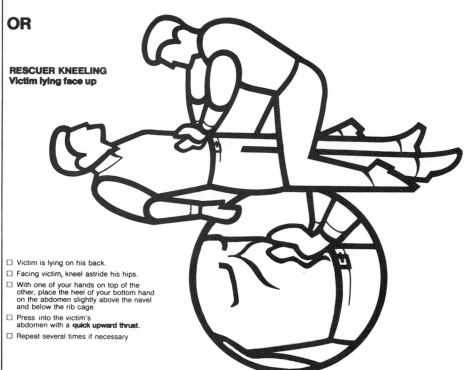

☐ Victim is lying on his back.

☐ Facing victim, kneel astride his hips.

☐ With one of your hands on top of the other, place the heel of your bottom hand on the abdomen slightly above the navel and below the rib cage.

☐ Press into the victim's abdomen with a **quick upward thrust.**

☐ Repeat several times if necessary

**EDUMED, INC.
BOX 52, CINCINNATI, OHIO 45201**

©EDUMED, INC. 1976   *T.M. PENDING

Figure 3.1.   Heimlich Maneuver. (*Posters, teaching slides, and wallet cards of the Heimlich Maneuver are now available. For information, send a stamped, self-addressed envelope to EDUMED, INC., Box 52, Cincinnati, Ohio 45201.*)

Never smoke, spit, or chew gum on the job.

Cover your face when you sneeze or cough.

Make use of a first aid kit immediately after an accidental cut or burn.

Stay at home if you are ill. A cold can be passed on to customers just by breathing on their food or utensils.

Use a clean fork or spoon for tasting food. To taste a liquid item, first ladle a small amount into a dish or saucer and then taste it.

Make certain that all equipment and utensils are clean and ready for use.

Use only clean and sanitary side towels.

Keep fingers to the edge of plates when serving.

Always carry clean tableware on a tray, a plate, or in a clean napkin.

Foot Care

Because service personnel are required to stand for such long periods at a stretch, special care must be taken to keep the feet and legs comfortable. Well-fitting, sturdy shoes will prove to be a worthwhile investment. Select shoes that have ample room for toe movement and provide adequate arch support. For extra comfort try wearing support hose. During long work periods, changing shoes and socks will refresh tired feet and the application of a foot powder or spray will help to reduce perspiration. After working hours, muscle tension can be relieved by that standby cure-all, a hot bath.

Dishwashing

Regular, effective cleaning of china, glassware, and silverware will prevent the spread of disease and infection. County, city, and state health regulations will vary from place to place. It is best to contact the local health department to establish dishwashing requirements, water properties, and temperature levels. If an automatic dishwashing machine is used, remember that it will maintain clean and sterile dishes only if it is operated properly. Certain basic steps must be followed in order to achieve clean dishes:

1. Scrape all dishes thoroughly.
2. Pre-rinse.
3. Stack the dishes ready for racking.
4. Rack but do not overload.
5. Invert cups, glasses, and bowls.
6. Wash silver in single layer.
7. Make sure enough detergent is used.
8. Check the temperature of the water — minimum of 140°F (60°C) for washing, and 180°F (82°C) for sterilization.
9. Drain, dry, and stack prior to storing in a clean cabinet.
10. Do not handle serviceware excessively.

Glass washing is, no doubt, the most difficult part of the dishwashing operation. If possible, run glassware through the machine first for best results, or have a separate washing operation. Prior to washing, look for lipstick or any other foreign material that is hard to remove.

Place silverware in warm water and detergent for pre-soaking in order to loosen any food particles. After this procedure, run it through the machine on a wire rack, in single layers for effective cleaning. Air-dry silverware and store it with the handles protruding to prevent excessive handling.

Replace all chipped or cracked china and glassware. Not only are they difficult to clean properly, but they may injure the patron as well.

After the completion of all dishwashing, the area around the dish table and the machine must be thoroughly cleaned. Screens, spray arms, and rinse pipes should be removed and also cleaned thoroughly. All water should be drained dry and the tank and machine properly cleaned inside and outside.

4
STYLES OF FOODSERVICE: OPERATIONS AND MENUS

The restaurant classifications offered here refer to the style of the operation. As these classifications are subjective, areas may overlap. The first three styles listed, *classic gourmet, grand luxe*, and *personality*, are primarily seated-service restaurants (with or without alcohol). The fourth, *reliability*, is usually a fast-food operation with a constant menu and dependable offerings. The fifth category, *filling station*, includes the commercial or industrial cafeteria and the institutional foodservice operation.

CLASSIC GOURMET RESTAURANT

The classic gourmet restaurant is refined and distinguished. A formally attired maitre d'hotel directs the dining experience with the assistance of appropriately attired captains, waiters, and buspersons. Designed to reflect the standards of the past, the classic gourmet restaurant is furnished with tabletops set with silver, china, linen, and crystal selected to accent the traditional decor.

Figure 4.1. The Palace, New York City— A Classic Gourmet Restaurant.

20

The classic menu offers a multi-course meal with an extensive assortment of foods and beverages. As quality is the keynote for the classic menu, reservations are essential to allow for the proper planning and preparation of food. Service is leisurely, although performed in a highly disciplined manner. Guests would not dine in this type of establishment if they wanted hurried service; the formal and elegant atmosphere suggests refinement and the fine food is meant to be savored slowly. Children would not be comfortable in these surroundings, as there are usually no provisions made for them.

GRAND LUXE RESTAURANT

The social developments of the seventies placed new demands on restaurateurs, who have tried to keep abreast of changing trends. Entertainment has become an important item in the restaurant industry since operations began using it to retain patrons for longer periods of time. Restaurants have begun to compete with the entertainment industry for the time and money of the American consumer. Eating out has become a night on the town in its own right instead of simply a prelude or conclusion to an evening's entertainment. Increasingly, the dining experience is designed to titillate all of the senses and not just the palate.

The atmosphere of a grand luxe restaurant is totally controlled. No details are left to the imagination. Every aspect of the interior is developed to create an ambience that overwhelms and transports the guest into the fabricated environment.

Consider one of the more successful restaurants of the 1970s, Windows on the World, high atop New York City's World Trade Center. From the lobby of the North Tower you are transported in a stainless steel cube 107 stories high in 58 seconds. The doors open on to a futuristic setting, complete with beautifully uniformed, attractive personnel. This interior is even more removed from the world below than the actual distance between them would allow one's imagination to believe. Proceeding through a mirrored passage decorated with large mineral crystals, you arrive at the restaurant where a panoramic view of New York City meets your eye, complete with the Statue of Liberty, the Empire State Building, and the Hudson River. You are seated in an area that is as much a showplace as it is a multileveled dining room.

The grand luxe restaurants evolved to meet the public's demand for elegant, imaginative foods and dining without the pomp and circumstance associated with the classical gourmet restaurants. Thus, a new blend of traditional table service with creative flair has developed, reducing and combining courses and introducing completely new service forms. Female maitre d's and captains, once unheard of, are being introduced in many restaurants with great success. Exciting new menus are being developed. Red wine with fish is no longer taboo. Salmon Bordelaise might even be offered on the menu. Innovations of all kinds are acceptable, with Nouvelle Cuisine selections listed comfortably alongside the classical items on a bill of fare.

One example of grand luxe dining can be found at The Box Tree in New York City. This elegant restaurant reduces the classical menu to four courses presented in a dining room that seats twenty-two. The appetizer and soup courses are combined by offering soup as an appetizer; the single cheese course is offered with the salad, eliminating the need for an extensive cheese cart.

Figure 4.2. Windows on the World, New York City—A Grand Luxe Restaurant.

Figure 4.3. Box Tree, New York City—A Grand Luxe Restaurant.

Figure 4.4. TGI Friday's, New York City—A Personality Restaurant.

Reinterpreting archaic foodservice techniques is not only exciting for the guest, it can also be economical for the operator. Benihana of Tokyo has perfected a meal that is both entertaining and inexpensive to serve. The food is prepared and served in front of the guests on a hibachi grill by a highly trained chef, eliminating the need for elaborate kitchen equipment and an extensive service staff.

PERSONALITY RESTAURANT

Personality restaurants may be high-, medium-, or low-priced operations. These establishments are essentially an extension of the owner-operator's personality. A sense of atmosphere is cultivated for its appeal to a particular clientele. The surroundings are pleasant and fashionable and the ambience is topical, in the current mode of the day. The mood is patron-oriented, with a convenient location, casual atmosphere, basic food, and friendly, familiar service.

Contemporary American dining breaks with European tradition in numerous ways. Menus usually stay within the boundaries of what has become basic American fare — steak, roast beef, fish and shellfish, potato, and salad. Patrons may be personally involved in

service, often slicing their own bread, preparing their own salads, and pouring beverages out of carafes.

Informality is in order. Reservations are seldom necessary except for peak periods. Patrons are seated on a first-come, first-served basis. Service is friendly and prompt, as many patrons wish to be in and out fairly quickly. The atmosphere, however, remains relaxed, with the decor varying from steel, glass, and chrome to exposed bricks, beams, and hanging plants. The life span of a personality operation can be as short as five or ten years. Trendy operations are highly subject to obsolescence, so their operators must strive to keep them alive and interesting.

RELIABILITY RESTAURANT

Reliability restaurants are the chain- or franchise-type of operation. Many American consumers, not very adventuresome in terms of food, look for something familiar such as the orange roof, golden arches, or starburst sign — anything that can be readily identified. Often the popularity of a familiar place is aided by the consistent quality of the foods offered. As long as the food is wholesome, clean, and filling, patrons will return for the dependable product at a reliable price.

The decor is never fancy for fear of intimidating the guest. Spotless facilities, clean rest rooms in bright colors, and easy access to main arteries or modes of transportation are of major importance to these operations.

FILLING STATION

The final category is the filling station, the institutional type of foodservice. These establishments service a "captive" clientele in schools, offices, factories, and hospitals. People patronize these operations when they are in a given place or situation and are looking for the most convenient, inexpensive mode of sustenance.

THE MENU

Menu is a French word that means "small list." It refers to the dishes offered, and to the actual printed list of these dishes. There are a variety of different styles of menus, each with its own content, each appropriate for a different type of foodservice establishment.

A *prix fixe* or fixed price menu charges one price for all meals. The guest selects one item for each course and pays a fixed price regardless of which entree is ordered.

Table d'hote literally means "from the table of the host." In Medieval times, travelers often took meals with the family that maintained the inn or home. The traveler ate as the host and family ate. Today, table d'hote refers to a menu that charges the price of a complete meal according to the entree selection.

The Medieval innkeeper soon found that by honoring special food requests he could command higher prices and generate greater revenues. This was the birth of the *a la carte* menu. The patron selects "from the card (or list)." Each food item is prepared and priced separately.

The *cycle menu* is a set of menus offered over a given period of time. At the end of the cycle, the series of menus is repeated or replaced with a new series. Cycle menus are designed to eliminate monotonous meals by preventing the same food item from being served on the same day of the following week. Cycle menus are usually offered in institutional settings, in plant or office buildings, and travel foodservices.

Special menus can be used for holidays or for specific groups of people such as children, low sodium dieters, and weight watchers. Room service menus in hotels and motels are usually specialty menus offering limited items.

The California menu originated in California with the birth of drive-in restaurants. It is a menu that does not change and is usually printed on stiff, durable paper or plastic, which can be hung on the wall. It differs from an ordinary menu in that it lists a variety of foods that are offered at any time during service. Customers can partake of a full meal, a partial meal, snack or fountain item during all hours of operation.

Figure 4.5. The Promenade at the World Trade Center, New York City — A Reliability Restaurant.

COMPOSITION OF THE MEAL

The Grand Couvert of Louis XIV and his court was the gastronomical zenith of western civilization and consisted of 250 to 500 separate dishes, all of them served at one affair. Such a display, by today's standards, would constitute sheer gluttony, and the Grand Couvert did in fact alter over the years not only for economic reasons, but out of consideration for cultural refinement.

Among his many culinary innovations, the famous chef Antoine Careme eliminated the need for so many food items. He reduced the meal to eight courses of eight dishes apiece, which still amounted to quite a lot of food. He compensated for this reduction visually, with the use of edible food displays and the introduction of pieces montees of ice and tallow sculpture.

The classical meal of today consists of nine separate courses: appetizer, soup, fish, intermezzo, entree, salad, cheese and fruit, dessert, and after-dinner beverages and tobacco.

Appetizer. Hot or cold appetizers, offered to titillate the taste buds, are usually prepared from shellfish, smoked meats and fish, fruits, vegetables, pates, caviar or other exotic and expensive ingredients. Portions are modest due to the high food cost and rich nature of these items. Quality ingredients should be used to establish the tone for a successful meal.

Soup. Soups can be categorized as clear or thick. Another mode of classification would be hot, cold, or jellied. One or two excellent offerings are more desirable than several mediocre ones. Preparation time and proper quantities are difficult to arrange with many soups on the menu. Specialty soup can be offered as an a la carte item. Avoid holding soup in a steam table, as the taste will quickly become inferior. Soups can be made to order in individual steam kettles or crocks. If large portions of soup are prepared, batch-heat fractional amounts at intervals throughout the meal period.

Poisson or fish course and releve. Traditionally the fish and the releve were offered separately, the releve acting as an intermediate light course between the fish and the main entree. Today one or the other is generally offered. Chicken, sweetbreads, or some other white meat usually constitutes the releve. The fish course and releve can be served hot or cold.

Intermezzo or sourbet. The sourbet is a pause between courses of a large meal to refresh the palate. Because alcohol rekindles hunger, an apple brandy called calvados was first used in France as the sourbet. Today unsugared fruit ices are commonly used. The serving of a sourbet also allows the kitchen to time the preparation of the following courses with greater accuracy.

Entree. The entree is the main course. Various types of hot entrees might be offered such as meat, offal, poultry, fish, seafood, game, or game birds. Cold entrees

Figure 4.6. Assorted Soup Bowls.

may consist of items such as fish, salads, or vegetable plates. Generally a vegetable and some type of starch accompany the entree. The accompaniments must be aesthetically planned to complement the color, contour, and texture of the entree. A well-planned plate needs no superfluous garnish.

Salad. Gastronomically speaking, lightly dressed greens should be taken after the entree, as greens naturally relax the stomach and help to lighten a heavy meal. In the United States, however, the salad with a heavier dressing is often served as a filler item before the entree.

Cheese and fruit. There are over four hundred varieties of cheese. Each is characterized by a particular flavor, texture, composition, size, and shape. Cheese is categorized as hard or soft depending on the amount of whey liquid left in the cheese, the manner of forming the curd, the bacteria or molds used, and the manner of curing. One good cheese is adequate, but an offering of four cheeses provides the proper color contrasts, contour differences, and flavor variations for the complete cheese board. Cheese may be accompanied by appropriate and well-ripened fruit. In Europe, where diners do not like to mix their courses, fruit and cheese are served separately.

Dessert. Desserts are popular menu items that prove to be quite profitable for the restaurant. As the appetizer sets the tone for the meal, the dessert brings the meal to completion. Desserts are meant, literally, to leave a sweet taste in the guest's mouth, and to provide stimulation after an extensive meal.

Beverages and tobacco. Some typical beverages taken at the end of a meal are coffee, tea, cordials, brandy and cognac, and special after-dinner drinks. As hot beverages tend to satisfy hunger and thus detract from further eating, they should be discouraged during the meal. The aroma of spicy essences and perfumes such as nard was used by the ancient Romans to induce a pleasant listlessness after a large meal. Today such an effect is produced by tobacco in the form of cigars and domestic or imported cigarettes.

Friands. Not actually a course, friands or lignappe are little extras given with the check. Petit fours, candies, mints and other sweets are, like dessert, literally intended to leave a good taste in the customer's mouth.

Variations

In practice, individual restaurants will deviate from the classical menu on the number of courses available, the makeup of each course, and the manner in which it is served. Soup, for example, might be offered as an appetizer, thus eliminating the need for a separate soup course. If fish is served as an entree, the fish course might be excluded from the meal. Cheese can be presented with the salad, again reducing the number of courses on the menu. Any number of variations can be developed to create imaginative, contemporary, and economical meals for today's palate.

COMPOSITION OF THE MENU

Creating a suitable menu demands considerable food knowledge. A variety of balanced alternatives must be offered that will appeal to the type of patron the restaurant is trying to attract. Numerous factors must be considered when composing a menu:

Preparation facilities and scope of equipment: A simple, well-produced meal is preferable to one that is elaborate but poorly prepared.

Service facilities: Take into account the number of service personnel and their level of training. The layout of the dining room and the type of tableware will also affect the foods served.

Costs: Compare the cost of food materials needed to produce the menu to the prices that will be charged. Raw food costs normally comprise from 20 to 40 percent of the meal price depending on the style of the restaurant and the type of service offered.

Meal period: The menu will vary with the time of day and the meal being served. Some food items are only appropriate for certain meals while others can be served at various hours.

Market: Bear in mind the type of guest likely to use the facilities at different time periods and for different meals. Also consider the number of guests and how long they will care to dine.

Balance: The menu must offer a balance of tastes, colors, textures, contours, nutritional values, prices, and methods of preparation.

Having established appropriate menu items, consider the frequency with which they are ordered. Perhaps more than one menu should be used. Be flexible enough to change the menu at regular intervals. However, while the menu must be extensive enough to offer the guest a variety of foods, it is advisable not to overload the menu. Large menus can confuse the patron. They also slow service by overburdening the kitchen as well as dining room staff. With too many selections on the menu some items will not move, resulting in inferior quality and, ultimately, increased waste.

A menu with fewer suggestions can be made more interesting if specials are featured. Specials based on seasonal or holiday food and beverage items will create menu excitement. The word "special" on the menu need not mean a reduced price. On the contrary, items that require more preparation and specific handling may command a higher price. Terminology such as "chef's suggestion" can also be used to denote unique or extra offerings. Items such as Crepe Suzette and Caesar Salad, which are difficult to prepare for only one person, can be listed as specials for two or more. Continental specials with a flair for showmanship can highlight certain categories of the menu. Special beverages lend style to the meal while increasing the check average.

Many restaurants feature specials on a daily, weekly, or seasonal basis. Variety in the menu is not only appealing to the guest, but also makes work more interesting for the staff. However, if the waiter is to effectively interpret the menu for the guest, he must be familiar with all specials, changes, or daily items like soup du jour. Management should inform the service staff of these items prior to service.

MENU DESIGN

The menu is the most important means of communication between kitchen and patron. It informs the customer of the food that is available and, depending on the establishment, facilitates the choice of meal by providing various balanced alternatives. In this capacity, a menu must measure up to the customer's expectations while arousing interest in the food items available.

As a self-service counter promotes impulse buying, so the visual appeal and persuasive food descriptions of a menu helps to sell food. This sales function of the menu is served through design. From the viewpoint of design, a menu must satisfy three main requirements:

The menu must be easy to handle in terms of size and layout.

Menu copy and prices must be clear, concise, and accurate. Descriptions must be easily under-

stood by the type of customer likely to use the restaurant.

The menu must be designed attractively and in keeping with the ambience of the operation.

Parts of the Menu

Whatever style or approach is used on the design, most menus have three main parts:

1. Listing of food categories. Common sense dictates that categories be listed in the order in which the meal is eaten. Never arrange the menu so that the categories do not follow in the proper sequence, even if such an arrangement appears graphically sound.

2. Individual food items. If foreign languages or unfamiliar terms are used, they should be defined or explained on the menu. If a small number of items require an explanation, the waiter may explain them verbally. This can be an excellent ice breaker for developing guest-waiter rapport. Verbal explanations should be kept to a minimum, however, as the guest is apt to forget too many of these items.

3. Descriptive copy. Writing a menu is a creative exercise — one that will take into account and reflect the nature of the clientele, the facility, and the writer. Inadvertently, the copy will express something of the writer's personal philosophy of food, and should therefore be well-planned.

The descriptive copy creates a verbal picture of what the guest is ordering. Words like "succulent," "freshly baked," or "golden brown" might be used, but not overworked. It is very important not to oversell an item lest the guest be unimpressed when it arrives. Rather, state the basics and delight the guest with a special presentation. The copy may include the origin of the dish and dominant flavorings, herbs, or spices; the method of preparation and accompanying sauce and garniture.

WORKING THE MENU AROUND THE CLOCK

There has been a break in tradition regarding the acceptable meal periods. As the American family unit continues to change, meals are being consumed less often with the total family. The size of meals has been decreasing while the frequency of eating increases. Dining habits are in a constant state of flux, and foodservice operators must keep abreast of the latest developments in the hospitality field in order to adequately serve the needs of their clientele.

Breakfast. Americans have tended to eat a light breakfast such as a donut, toast, or breakfast roll with coffee or tea. Today's diet-conscious customers are now eating more fresh fruits, yogurts, and whole grain cereals and breads. Higher income items like pancakes or table d'hote breakfasts should get a special position on the menu to attract attention. Numbered breakfasts facilitate ordering by the guest and order-taking by the service personnel. The number of menu items is an important factor to remember — one which should be dictated by the demands of your clientele. Alcoholic beverages such as Bloody Marys and Screwdrivers are commonly offered with breakfast in many metropolitan areas.

Brunch. Brunch combines a late breakfast and an early lunch, and thus serves all manner of appetites. For many guests, it will be the first food they have had since rising. Others, who may have eaten a very light breakfast, will be inclined to order luncheon items. The brunch menu should include a good mix of imaginative breakfast–lunch items. Brunch patrons might be induced to order a cocktail such as the Ramos Gin Fizz, Brandy Milk Punch, or that classic standby, the Bloody Mary. Champagne or white wine is also suitable. Main dishes can be substantial, since the brunch patron may eliminate the luncheon meal.

Lunch. Luncheon menus should contain a good selection of menu items, possibly including a la carte and table d'hote meals and sandwiches. Prepared specials can expedite service for the hurried guest. The luncheon menu can correlate directly to the dinner menu, keeping foods fresh and minimizing leftovers. Alcoholic beverages are in good order, with the current trend away from spirits and toward increased sales in wines and beer.

Afternoon menus. Afternoon menus can generate revenue during an ordinarily slow period. Tea and coffee with confections are popular for an afternoon coffee break. Happy hours with snack-type food giveaways can stimulate bar sales.

Dinner menu. Creative dinner menus are the vitality of a foodservice operation. Small menus that change frequently or that create menu excitement by offering speciality or ethnic dishes are currently successful. Exceptional quality and flavor are essential for every item offered on a limited menu.

Supper. Supper is offered after the dinner hour in metropolitan areas where there is a concentration of cultural entertainment or sporting events. The supper menu is smaller and easier to prepare than the dinner menu, thereby cutting expenses and eliminating the need for a large staff. Supper clubs are enjoying renewed popularity after a slow period during the 1960s.

Late snacks. Many hotels and motels now feature full-length, first-run films on television sets. To accommodate the night owl types, deli plates are offered with a selection of cheeses, meats, and snack foods served with beer or wine. These items can be prepared during a regular shift and held in refrigeration for service all night.

5
PREPARING FOR SERVICE

DINING ROOM MISE EN PLACE

The first step toward becoming a dining room professional is the regular, conscientious performance of *mise en place*. This French phrase literally means "to put in place." In the foodservice industry, mise en place is generally understood to mean the organization and completion of all the duties and tasks one must perform to carry out the job at hand smoothly and efficiently.

The mise en place of the opening dining room crew would include setting up the dining room and insuring that everything used for service is readily available and easily accessible. Once service begins, personnel must be able to devote their full attention to the immediate demands of serving the guests. Time cannot be wasted preparing equipment and supplies that could have been organized and made ready earlier. Particular tasks to be performed as part of the opening mise en place are:

Checking reservation book
Arranging tables and chairs
Laying tablecloths
Folding napkins
Checking flatware, china, and glasses
Setting tables
Stocking sidestands
Adjusting temperature and lighting

The duties of the closing dining room crew should be coordinated with the responsibilities of the opening crew. While the opening crew sets up the dining room, the closing crew cleans up and restocks the dining room for the next day. The mise en place of the closing crew might include:

Returning all foodstuffs to the kitchen
Clearing tables
Stacking chairs
Cleaning, refilling, and refrigerating condiments
Replenishing china, glassware, and flatware
Cleaning shelves and trays
Adjusting lighting and temperature

Many establishments make use of an opening and closing checklist. Among the items included on such a list are:

China	Pitchers
Silver	Pantry
Glasses	Creamers
Condiments	Floor
Garbage	Coffee Equipment
Side stands	Soup cart
Tray stands	Gueridons
Trays	Trolleys
Tables	Displays
Chairs	Rechauds
Back room	Linen
Temperature	Refrigerator
Lighting	Menus

LINEN

Table linen as we know it now represents centuries of evolution. Napkins are known to have been used as early as Roman times. Guests in ancient Rome brought their own napkins, tying one under the chin and keeping another nearby for wiping the fingers, which were used instead of a fork.

In feudal times small tablecloths were used, but only to cover the host's place. By the Middle Ages full tablecloths were common. At large banquets the table-cloth would be changed several times. It was not long before the runner was introduced — a long, narrow strip of linen laid along the edge of the table. The runner was used by guests to wipe their fingers and mouths. Later came the *touaille*. This roller-type towel was fixed to the wall and used by several diners.

In the sixteenth century the individual napkin, not seen since Roman times, came back into fashion. The napkin was draped over the left arm, but when large, starched, ruffled collars came into style, the napkin was tied around the neck to prevent soiling the collar. As an insignia of station, the maitre d'hotel carried a napkin rolled in an epaulet on his left shoulder.

The royal forks and knives were often wrapped in a napkin and placed in a nef or golden vessel. From this tradition the French introduced elaborate napkin folds. The *serviette*, as the napkin was called, was changed at each course of the meal, and was sometimes scented with perfume.

Napkin folds have been used in the dining room for ornamentation. At times, food may even be served in the pocket of a folded napkin. This is known as *a la serviette*, as in truffles a la serviette.

Linen Selection

Until modern times, tablecloths and napkins were traditionally made of linen, a natural fiber produced from flax. Today man-made fibers are often substituted for natural ones, but the term "linen" still applies in a general sense to all fabrics used at table.

Several items must be considered in the selection of a fabric for the tabletop. The style and decor of the dining room will dictate the color, pattern, closeness of weave, and texture chosen. Consider also the service-ability of the fabric. Can it be easily mended? Will the edges soon become frayed? Choose a fabric that is attractive and economically suitable.

Colored cloths are often selected for decorative purposes. While colored cloths generally show less spotting, they are more difficult to launder, repair, and replace than white cloths. In addition, colored cloths may fade and create an uneven look in the dining room. When there is need for color or contrast, a coarse, colored cloth can be used over a white undercloth. Another alternative is to use placemats or colored napkins on top of a white tablecloth.

Napkins. Place napkins to the left of the fork and one inch from the edge of the table, or in the middle of the place setting, directly in front of the guest. Large dinner-sized paper napkins are treated as linen napkins. Dispenser napkins should be left in the dispenser. Cloth napkins are usually folded in the style of the house. Some folds allow a place for dinner rolls, bread, or a small bouquet of flowers. There are countless napkin folds. The choice will depend on the ambience and decor of the dining room, the skill of the staff, the time

Figure 5.1. Simple Flat Fold.

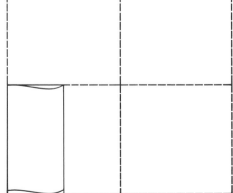

Step a. Unfold square napkin.   **Step b.** Fold in quarters.   **Step c.** Fold once from right to left. Avoid exposing as much of the hem as possible.

Figure 5.2. Double Pointed Flat Fold.

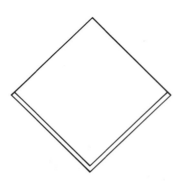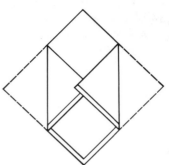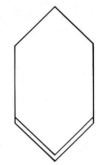

Step a. Fold in quarters.

Step b. Rotate counterclockwise 45 degrees.

Step c. Fold left point into center. Fold right point into center.

Step d. Turn over.

Figure 5.3. Pentagon.

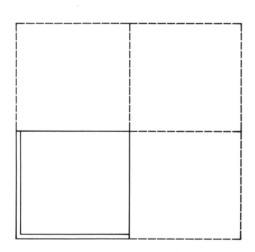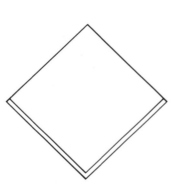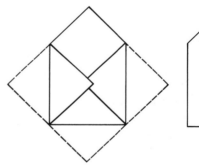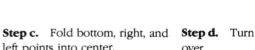

Step a. Fold napkin in quarters.

Step b. Rotate counterclockwise 45 degrees.

Step c. Fold bottom, right, and left points into center.

Step d. Turn over.

available to actually do the folding, and the other table top items. Generally speaking, the trend is toward simple table settings that are not suited to the involved, archaic, and elaborate folds of the past. Uncomplicated folds take less time and create a mood of simple elegance.

As linen is usually delivered to the dining room already folded, try to use the existing fold as a starting point. This will save time and eliminate the need of having to work around the existing crease. After repeated use, the edges of cloth napkins tend to become uneven. Also, the stitching around the edges can be unsightly. If possible, choose a fold that will avoid exposing the edges of the napkin.

Silence cloth. A silence cloth is often used under the tablecloth to cushion the noise of plates and cutlery placed on the table during service. Some tables have permanent cushioning on the tabletop to serve as a silencer. Another tablecloth or a thin piece of foam rubber or felt can be used as a silence cloth. Besides preventing noise, a silence cloth protects the tabletop, soaks up spills, and prevents the top cloth from sliding.

Figure 5.4. Accordion.

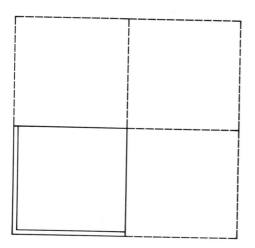

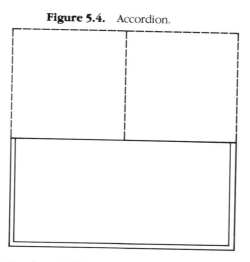

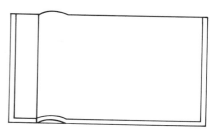

Step a. Fold napkin in quarters.

Step b. Unfold in half from left to right.

Step c. Grasp the top and bottom of the napkin a few inches from the left edge. Overlap the napkin to the left.

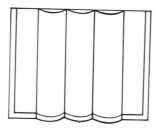

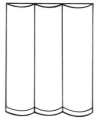

Step d. Repeat twice more.

Step e. Tuck right and left edges under.

Tablecloths. Inspect all tablecloths before using them in the dining room. Turn in all that are soiled, stained, shredded, or torn to the supervisor. Before laying a tablecloth, certain preparations should be made:

Clean the tabletops.

Level the tables by turning screw cleats on the base of adjustable tables or by inserting pieces of cork under legs of nonadjustable tables (never use matchbooks), and tighten center bolt of pedestal tables.

Spread and secure silence cloth or undercloth.

Smooth any creases and make sure cloths are centered.

The center crease of all tablecloths in the dining room should point up and run in the same direction, generally toward the entrance. This practice gives an organized look to the room, especially when the tables are not occupied. When a tablecloth becomes soiled during service, change it. Never shake out a tablecloth in the dining room. This distracts the guest, is unsanitary, and indicates poor training. During service, bare tabletops should never be exposed. Some operations use an undercloth to avoid completely stripping the table when it is time to replace the tablecloth.

Figure 5.5. Laying a Tablecloth.

Step a. Place the folded tablecloth in the center of the table.

Step b. Unfold it in sections evenly across the table. The tablecloth should now be in three sections with the center crease and the two hems facing you.

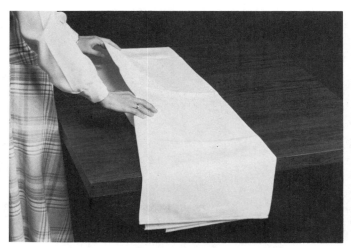

Step c. Hold the center crease and the first hem between your index and middle fingers.

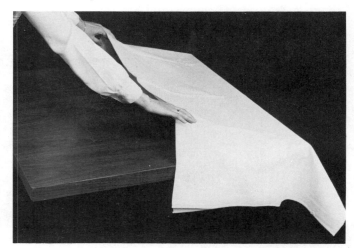

Step d. Gently flick your wrist. The bottom hem will unfold over the far edge of the table.

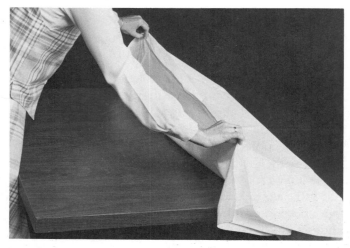

Step e. Grasp the remaining hem with the thumb and index finger. Use your middle finger to hold the hem and center crease together.

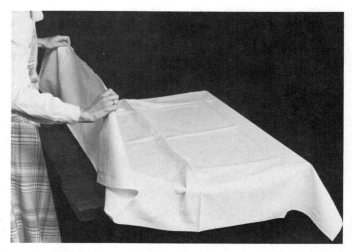

Step f. Pull the bottom hem toward you while releasing the center crease. The tablecloth will unfold with the center crease pointing upward.

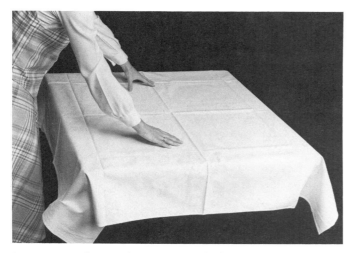

Step g. Straighten and center the tablecloth.

Step h. Adjust the overhanging edges.

Figure 5.6. Changing a Tablecloth.

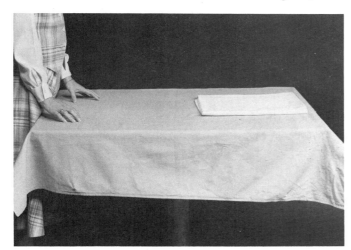

Step a. Place a clean, folded tablecloth slightly beyond the center of the table.

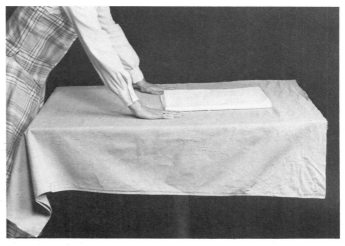

Step b. Pull the soiled tablecloth toward you so the far hem is even with the edge of the table.

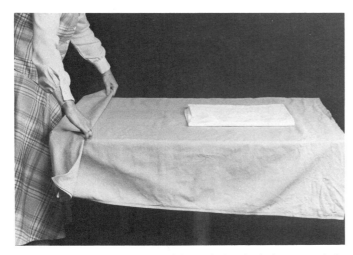

Step c. Fold the closest end of the soiled tablecloth even with the edge of the table.

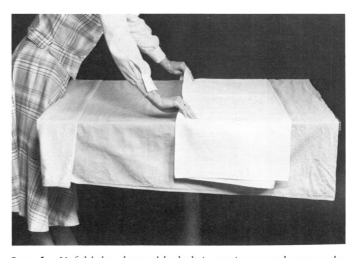

Step d. Unfold the clean tablecloth in sections evenly across the table.

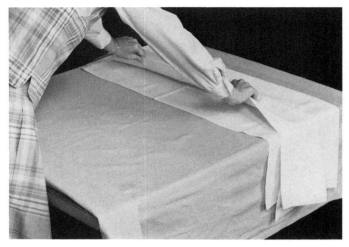

Step e. The tablecloth should now be in three sections with the center crease and two hems facing you.

Step f. Hold the center crease between your middle and index fingers. Hold the first hem between your index finger and thumb.

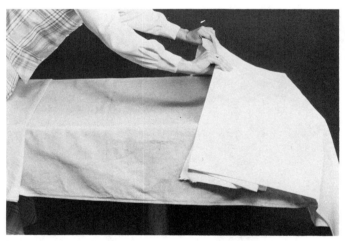

Step g. Gently flick your wrist. The bottom hem will unfold over the far edge of the table.

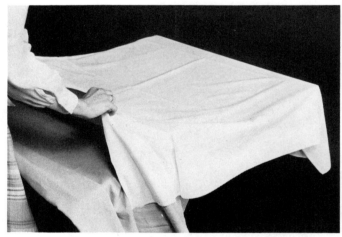

Step h. Pull the clean tablecloth toward you. The soiled tablecloth will begin to slide toward you.

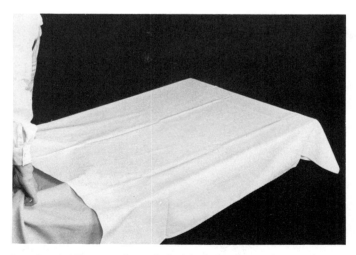

Step i. Swiftly grasp the soiled tablecloth as you release the clean one. Slide the soiled tablecloth off the table.

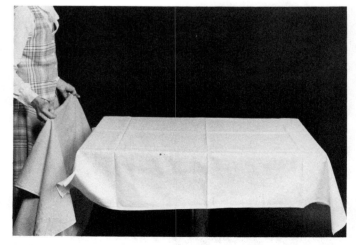

Step j. The clean tablecloth should be covering the table and the soiled tablecloth should be in your hand.

Step k. Adjust and straighten the overhanging edges.

SERVICEWARE

Serviceware is a general term for all utensils and wares used in the dining room to serve the guest, in addition to certain kitchen utensils such as carving knives and forks, ladles, and perforated spoons. The main classifications of serviceware are:

Flatware: knives, forks and spoons, regardless of style or usage

China: plates of all sizes, dishes, cups, saucers, underliners

Glassware: items such as glass decanters, carafes, pitchers, and all drinking vessels used at table or at bar for beer, wine, and cocktails

Holloware: technically, those service items of significant depth or volume; more generally, large service items including platters, trays, stands, etc.

One of the first things the patron will notice on entering the dining room is the tabletop design. For this reason, serviceware must be compatible with the overall design and motif of the operation. Unless service items are selected with regard to simplicity and completeness of detail, the effect created in the dining room will be one of disarray, confusion, and poor taste.

In selecting serviceware other qualities to consider aside from the aesthetics are:

Durability: Will the item selected stand up to the wear and tear of daily use?

Cleanability: Will the item be able to be cleaned with the sanitation capabilities of the operation without excessive time and effort?

Economy: Is the item affordable?

Flatware

Spoons were used by both the ancient Egyptians and Romans. During the Middle Ages, general-purpose knives were carried by most guests, and spoons were fairly common. The dinner fork was not widely used until the eighteenth century, but it had been used as a kitchen implement. The Greeks and Italians were the first Europeans to use the dinner fork, in the sixteenth and seventeenth centuries. Catherine de Medici took her cooks and kitchen implements with her when she traveled to France from Italy in 1533 to marry the Dauphin, but the fork did not gain immediate acceptance. Seventy years later, the traveler Tom Coryat introduced the fork to the nobility in England, but again it did not become fashionable. For the next hundred years, Europeans continued to eat with their fingers. As late as 1897, sailors in the British Navy were not permitted to use forks as the use of these items was considered an affectation. Today we not only have knives, forks, and spoons, but we employ many variations of these pieces for specific food items.

Several considerations must be made prior to selecting flatware:

Quality: Composition and finishing plate should be of quality appropriate to establishment's overall standards.

Balance: Sizes, proportions, and weights should be attractive and comfortable to use.

Design: Flatware design should reflect establishment's ambience.

Durability: Flatware should be chosen with regard to the use and to methods of handling and washing.

Stackability: Nesting should be possible with minimum of scratching.

Knife edge: Knives should retain sharpness of edges and serrations.

Handles: Materials used may be nylon, xylonite, compressed wood, solid steel, or hollow plate. Flatware may be one solid piece or have handles fitted with a bolster or rivets.

Figure 5.7. Assorted Flatware. Bottom Row (left to right): Cocktail Fork, Three-Tine Dinner (Fish) Fork, Salad Fork, Dinner Fork, Butter Spreader, Dinner Knife, Fish Knife, Steak Knife, Cheese Knife.

Top Row: Oval Bowl Soup Spoon, Parfait Spoon, Bouillon Spoon, Tablespoon, Grapefruit Spoon, Sugar Spoon, Dessert Spoon, Escargot Fork.

Care of Flatware

Stainless steel and silver require distinctly different cleaning methods. To clean stainless flatware, presoak all pieces, especially when stubborn stains occur. Never use an abrasive scrubbing pad as it will mar the finish. Wash pieces in hot water and detergent, then rinse in hot water of at least 180°F (82.2°C).

Cleaning silver does not have to be a long and tedious job; it can be done simply and quickly. Wash all silver in sudsy water as soon as possible after use: never soak silver. A few drops of ammonia added to the soapy water will cut through residue and add to brightness. Immediately after washing, rinse thoroughly and wipe dry with a soft clean cloth. To polish, rub the silver with a good paste or liquid polish, using a soft clean cloth. For quicker polishing, use a treated silver cloth. Buff with a dry soft cloth.

Clean silver should not be touched by bare hands

as grease from hands causes new tarnish spots. Do not bundle silver with elastic or rubber bands; these contain sulphur and will leave dark marks. To prevent tarnish, wrap silver pieces in anti-tarnish cloth and store in an airtight place.

Detarnishing baths are not for silver pieces with designs in high relief — that is, pieces in which the crevices should remain dark. These baths are for fast, easy cleaning of smooth-surfaced silver. Use a large aluminum pan with enough water to cover the silver. For each quart of water, add one teaspoon of baking soda. Bring the solution to a boil, then turn off the heat. Add the silver and let stand a few minutes. Remove the silver, wash it in hot sudsy water, rinse, and wipe dry. The aluminum sets up an electrolytic reaction with silver sulfide and removes the tarnish. The aluminum pan will need to be scoured with a soapy steel-wool pad, or boiled in a solution of vinegar or cream of tartar and water.

China

Centuries ago primitive man discovered that certain types of soil, when mixed with water and worked with the hands, could be formed into desired shapes. When laid on a rock in the full rays of the sun, these shapes hardened and could hold water. When these forms were dried near or in a fire, the resulting dish (from the Latin *discus* via Old English *disc*) lasted longer, absorbed water less readily, and gave less off-flavors to the item it held. Regular ovens or kilns were invented to produce assorted wares. Each district produced a different colored ware, depending on the type of clay available; hence the colored decorations of today.

In the course of history many types of wares have been developed, each employing different mixtures of clay, feldspar, flint, and sometimes bone, each fired (heated to redness) at a different temperature. Those items fired at the upper temperature range become completely vitrified — nonporous, dense, practically non-absorbent. Those fired only enough to harden are porous, with large interstices that permit air or liquids to pass through them. Thus, the characteristics of a given piece will be determined by its composition and firing temperature.

Terra cotta: usually unglazed, relatively soft, and very porous. A familiar example of terra cotta is a common flower pot.

Stoneware: usually white, somewhat porous, and frequently has a transparent glaze.

Pottery: generally glazed. Pottery has large pores but does not absorb much liquid.

Porcelain: glazed and nonporous. Porcelain's texture is quite fine and has a ring when tapped.

Most restaurant china manufactured today has been vitrified. Fired at very high temperatures, this china

Figure 5.8.   Assorted China. Bottom Row (left to right): Tea or Coffee Cup, Soup Plate, Bouillon Cup, Handled Bouillon Cup. Top Row: Demi-Tasse Cup, Mug, Crock, Petite Marmite.

becomes more durable, easier to clean, and able to withstand relatively high heat and extreme cold.

It was the custom during Medieval times for two people to share a *trencher*, a stale piece of bread with the center hollowed out to hold stewed meats and juices. The trencher was not eaten but thrown to the dogs. Today we are more refined. We not only have our own dinner plates, but many food items require special servicewares of their own as well. There are countless shapes and sizes of restaurant china with varied usage. As with other equipment, the particular pieces used at a given establishment will be determined by the individual needs of the operation.

Glassware

Glass is produced by heating sand (silicon dioxide) and other substances to a very high temperature. The molten mass is blown or molded into shape and then allowed to cool and solidify by carefully regulating the temperature. This process is called annealing. Handles and other parts are attached by welding during this process.

When selecting the proper glassware, the following considerations should be made:

Range: When possible, order multipurpose stocks.

Designs: Coordinate glassware with other dining room equipment.

Serviceability: Smooth, simple, robust shapes are preferred. Consider the width of the opening for proper drinking, washing, draining, drying, pouring, and stacking.

Manufacture: Examine the clarity of glass. Inspect for cracks, faults, bubbles, and distortions.

Replacement: Are additional supplies readily available?

Glasses can occupy a large surface area, so give special consideration to storage requirements for stocking glasses and for service needs in the bar and dining areas. Specially designed hanging racks and trays may be used for glasses to facilitate storing and handling.

Holloware

Holloware pieces used in the dining room are usually specialty items: tea and coffee sets, covered serving dishes, tureens and bowls, ice buckets, oval platters and trays, cafe diable sets, chafing dishes, punch bowls, supreme sets, and the like. If covers are provided, be sure they fit well and are preferably interchangeable with other serviceware. Component pieces may be sold separately or in sets, one example being a soup tureen with or without a cover. In using holloware, make provisions for the appropriate accompanying serving utensils, such as spoons and ladles.

Often holloware is made from some form of metal. Metal items are stronger and better able than ceramic items to withstand the impact and stress arising from frequent handling. In addition, the weight of a large metalware dish can be appreciably lighter than ceramic, and a greater variety of shapes is available. Metal food containers can create problems, however. Certain metals can taint foods, and food containing acids and alkalines

Figure 5.9.   Overhead Glass Rack at Windows on the World, New York City.

Figure 5.10. Stemmed Coupe and Parfait Dishes.

Figure 5.11. Water Pitchers.

Figure 5.12. Coffee Pots.

Figure 5.13. Teapot and Hot Water Pot.

Figure 5.14. Supreme Set in Three Pieces.

Figure 5.15. Supreme Set Assembled.

Figure 5.16.   Silver Service Platters.

Figure 5.17.   Seafood Server.

Figure 5.18.   Fruit Salad Bowl and Shrimp Server.

Figure 5.19.   Divided Vegetable Dish.

Figure 5.20.   Covered Ceramic Tureen and Ladle.

Figure 5.21.   Covered Escoffier Dish.

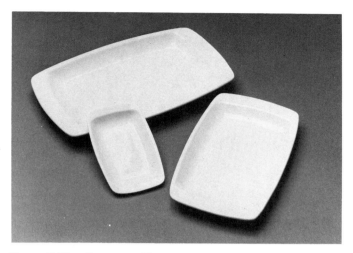

Figure 5.22. Pyroceram Platters.

Figure 5.23. Gooseneck.

Figure 5.24. Candelabra and Candlestick.

Figure 5.25. Sous Cloche.

Figure 5.26. Serving Bowl.

Figure 5.27. Compote Stand for Fruits, Nuts, and Sweets.

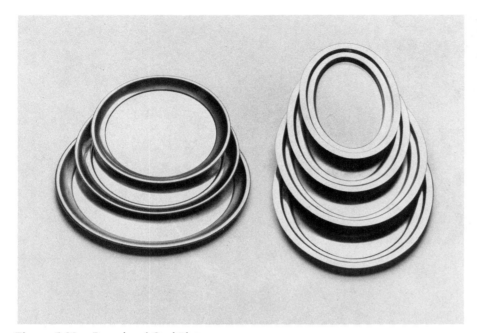

Figure 5.28.   Round and Oval Platters.

Figure 5.29.   Bud Vase.

can corrode metals. Difficulties also arise in washing, polishing, and maintaining the appearance of metalware.

SETTING THE TABLE

Like first impressions of people, the guest's first impression of the dining room — the individual tables and the appearance they give together — will dramatically effect the guest's dining experience. Proper table setting involves a number of elements. The cover, the flatware or silverware, the glassware and the china: all require careful attention if the truly professional dining experience is to be achieved.

The Cover

The term "cover" or *couvert* has two distinct meanings in the dining room. "Cover" can refer to the number of guests in a dining room or at a table. For example, "The dining room will seat 75 covers," or "This table will seat eight covers comfortably." The place setting that is laid according to the type of meal and service is also called a "cover." It denotes the flatware, glassware, and china that are set for the guest. It is this second meaning of cover that will be expanded here.

Table arrangements should be neat and symmetrically balanced. Set all tables identically for a uniform, stylized appearance. Whenever possible, position

place settings so that guests face each other. To provide adequate room for each guest, allow a minimum of eighteen inches for each setting.

Settings on deuces may be positioned banquette-style (side by side) or at right angles to allow the guest to face the dining room. Never have deuces facing a blank wall. On rectangular or square tables, the bottom edge of all flatware, napkins, and cover plates should be in a straight line, one inch from the edge of the table. On round tables, these items may be placed in a straight line, or they may follow the rim of the table. To assure neat, symmetrical, and uniform table-top arrangements, certain guidelines should be followed. These are detailed in the next few paragraphs.

Flatware

Check flatware for spots prior to service, and return them to dish room if soiled. Forks are placed to the left with the tines facing up or, for a continental touch, with the tines facing down. Oyster or cocktail forks may be placed on the right side or they can be served on the underliner with the food item. Spoons are placed on the right side, face up. Knives are placed on the right with the cutting edge facing to the left.

Whenever possible, only set those pieces that are required by the food to be served. Do not set more than six pieces of flatware at a time except where a cocktail fork is used. If the menu calls for more, it is best to place the dessert utensils at the time of service, or to place

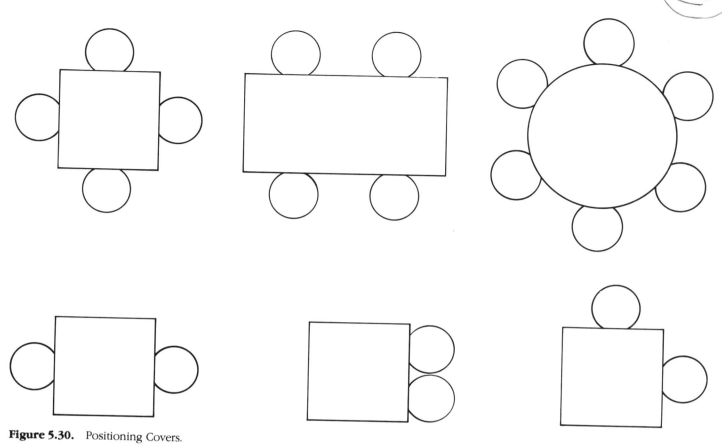

Figure 5.30. Positioning Covers.

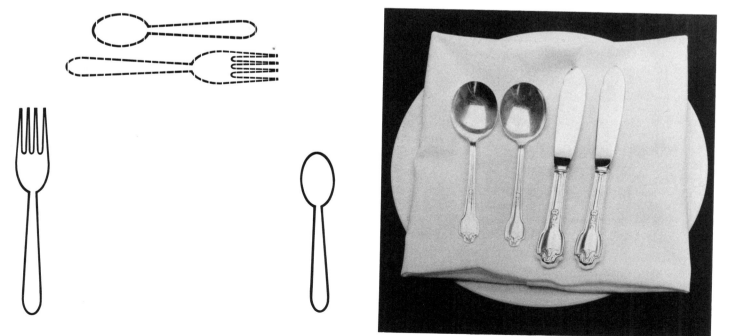

Figure 5.31. Dessert Flatware.

Figure 5.32. Flatware on Linen on Dinner Plate.

them above the cover. Flatware positioned above the cover plate should be moved to the correct position by the service person before the appropriate course.

Position flatware in the order in which it is to be used; for example, utensils to be used first are placed on the outside, with flatware for the succeeding courses placed towards the center of the cover.

Carry all clean flatware to the table on a dinner plate with a clean linen napkin. Place flatware three-fourths of an inch from the showplate.

China and Glassware

Place the bread and butter plate to the left of the cover above the tines of the fork. Place the bread and butter knife on the right hand edge of the plate, with the blade of the knife facing left.

Figure 5.33. Glass Placement.

Place the coffee cup and saucer, whether preset or added to the service during the meal, to the right of the cover. Position the top of the saucer in line with the top of the adjacent piece of flatware. The handle should be pointing to the right and set at a slight angle toward the edge of the table. This positioning allows the guest to grasp the cup handle with ease.

When emblems, logos, or names are on service plates place them towards the guest.

Position glassware to the right of the cover above the point of the dinner knife. If more than one glass is to be set, such as a white wine glass, a red wine glass, and a champagne glass, position them at an angle up from the point of the dinner knife in order of service from right to left. If the red wine is to be served after the white wine, place it to the left and slightly above the white wine glass.

If a water glass is to accompany the wine glasses, it is generally placed just above the dinner knife with the wine glasses angled slightly above and to the left. In Europe, it is common to place the water glass to the left and slightly above the wine glasses with the champagne, tulip, or port glass positioned to the left of the water glass. (For additional information on glassware see chapter 7.)

Standard Covers

The following are descriptions of standard covers for restaurant foodservice.

Simple cover: includes only the bare essentials.

A la carte cover: used for French or Russian service. Additional serviceware is placed prior to the appropriate course.

Full dinner cover: used for American, banquet, butler, and English service. All serviceware is placed on the table before the guests arrive. Serviceware set will be determined by the menu items.

Dinner cover with a fish course: a full dinner cover with the addition of a fish fork and knife.

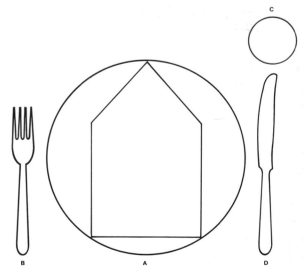

Figure 5.34. Simple Cover. (A) Service Plate and Napkin, (B) Dinner Fork, (C) All-Purpose Wine Glass, (D) Dinner Knife.

Figure 5.35. A La Carte Cover. (A) Service Plate and Napkin, (B) Dinner Fork, (C) Bread and Butter Plate with Butter Spreader, (D) Red Wine Glass, (E) White Wine Glass, (F) Dinner Knife.

Figure 5.36. Complete Dinner Cover for American Service. (A) Service Plate and Napkin, (B) Salad Fork, (C) Dinner Fork, (D) Bread and Butter Plate with Butter Spreader, (E) Dessert Spoon and Fork, (F) Red Wine Glass, (G) White Wine Glass, (H) Bouillon Spoon, (I) Dinner Knife.

Figure 5.37. Complete Dinner Cover with Fish Course. (A) Service Plate and Napkin, (B) Salad Fork, (C) Dinner Fork, (D) Fish Fork, (E) Bread and Butter Plate with Butter Spreader, (F) Dessert Spoon and Fork, (G) Red Wine Glass, (H) White Wine Glass, (I) Bouillon Spoon, (J) Fish Knife, (K) Dinner Knife.

Lobster cover: all the necessary serviceware for lobster service.

Standard dinner cover with seafood appetizer: a standard dinner cover with the addition of utensils for shrimp or seafood cocktail, oysters, or clams on a half shell.

Standard dinner cover with escargot appetizer: a standard dinner cover with the addition of snail pinchers and a snail fork.

Omelette cover: the bare essentials for an omelette.

Spaghetti cover: a simple setting with the addition of parmesan cheese.

Here are some additional cover suggestions for specific menu items:

Artichoke (whole): dinner plate, dinner fork on right, finger bowl set up, small plate for leaves.

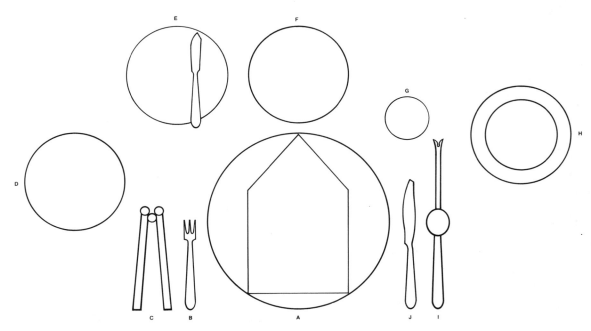

Figure 5.38. Lobster Cover. (A) Service Plate and Napkin, (B) Cocktail Fork, (C) Lobster Cracker, (D) Small Bowl of Melted Butter, (E) Bread and Butter Plate with Butter Spreader, (F) Small Plate for Shells, (G) White Wine Glass, (H) Fingerbowl Setup, (I) Lobster Pick, (J) Fish Knife.

Figure 5.39. Standard Cover with Seafood Appetizer. (A) Service Plate and Napkin, (B) Salad Fork, (C) Dinner Fork, (D) Oyster Setup (Crackers, Horseradish, Tabasco), (E) Bread and Butter Plate with Butter Spreader, (F) Red Wine Glass, (G) White Wine Glass, (H) Cocktail Fork, (I) Bouillon Spoon, (J) Dinner Knife.

Asparagus Stalks: dinner plate, dinner fork on the right, finger bowl set up.

Bouillabaisse: large soup plate on a large underliner, soup spoon, ladle (if served in tureen), small plate for waste products.

Caviar: small chilled plate, small knife or butter spreader, toast basket, butter dish.

Cheese: small plate, small fork, small knife.

Dessert (pastry): dessert fork and spoon, soup spoon for cutting pastry, small plate.

Dessert (coupe): underliner, coupe glass, paper doily between coupe glass and underliner, teaspoon for coupe, teaspoon for hot beverage.

Figure 5.40. Escargot Cover. (A) Service Plate and Napkin, (B) Salad Fork, (C) Dinner Fork, (D) Snail Pinchers, (E) Bread and Butter Plate with Butter Spreader, (F) Red Wine Glass, (G) White Wine Glass, (H) Cocktail Fork, (I) Bouillon Spoon, (J) Dinner Knife.

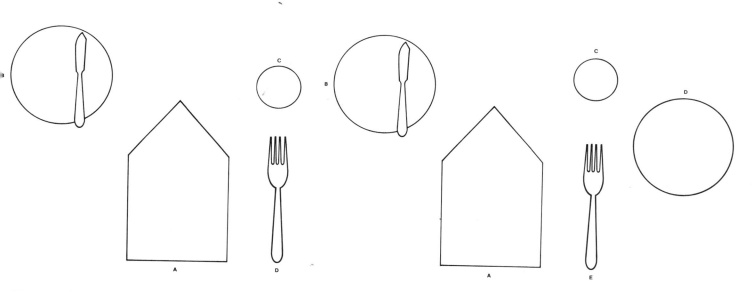

Figure 5.41. Supper Omelette Cover. (A) Napkin, (B) Bread and Butter Plate with Butter Spreader, (C) All-Purpose Wine Glass, (D) Dinner Fork.

Figure 5.42. Pasta Cover. (A) Napkin, (B) Bread and Butter Plate with Butter Spreader, (C) All-Purpose Wine Glass, (D) Cup of Grated Cheese on Underliner, (E) Dinner Fork.

Fruit Basket: small plate, small knife and small fork, finger bowl set up, large bowl of fresh water to wash certain fruits.

Half Grapefruit: teaspoon, sugar, small bowl on underliner.

Melon: dessert spoon, appropriate-sized small bowl on an underliner.

Hors d'oeuvre: large service plate, small fork, small knife.

Melon and Prosciutto: slice of melon, with or without rind, finely sliced prosciutto, small plate, small knife, small fork.

Pate: small plate, small knife, small fork, toast and butter.

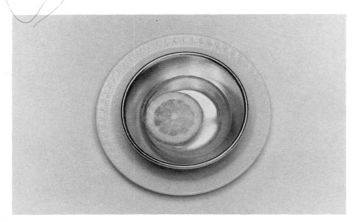

Figure 5.43. Fingerbowl with Warm Water and Slice of Lemon.

Figure 5.45. Sugar Packet Holder and Sugar Pourer.

Finger Bowl: finger bowl filled to 1/3 with warm water, slice of lemon in water, underliner, paper doily between underliner and finger bowl.

SIDE STAND

The side stand is the service station for the dining room. It should be cleaned and well stocked with all necessary materials before service. Proper use of the side stand will minimize the number of trips to the kitchen for stock items. A side stand might include all necessary flatware, wine lists, glassware, ashtrays, condiments, sterno, china, paper goods, coffee cups and saucers, napkins, tablecloths, perhaps a coffee warmer unit, a menu rack, and a compartment for personal belongings. Because it holds so many different items, the side stand must be well organized or else it will hinder rather than facilitate service.

Figure 5.46. Salt and Pepper Holder.

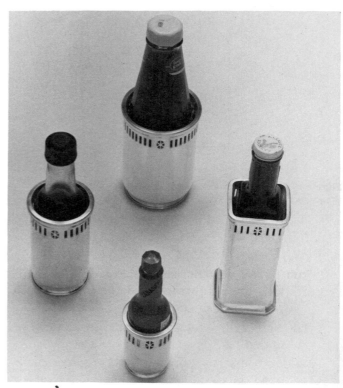

Figure 5.44. Vinegar and Oil Cruets.

Figure 5.47. Condiments in Holders.

Other items that might be included on a side stand are:

Bread baskets	Wine coolers
Set up for crumbing tables	Matches
Flower vases	Oyster sets
Doilies	Jams and jellies
Finger bowls	Sugar and sweetner refills
Lobster and escargot equipment	Placemats

Miscellaneous edible items like ice, coffee, butter, cream, rolls, breads, and garnishes can also be stored in the dining room side stand. However, to insure freshness and for optimum control, it is recommended that these food items be dispensed by food personnel from the kitchen, rather than by service personnel in the dining room.

Special attention should be given to stocking the side stand with "drugstore" items such as condiments, oil and vinegar cruets, salt and pepper, catsup, bottled sauces, or mustards. Edibles should be handled in the following manner:

1. Remove storeroom prices.
2. Refill half-empties.
3. Clean the cover, rim, and body of all jars and containers.
4. Soak lids and wipe dry.
5. Store on a clean rack or tray.
6. Refrigerate open bottles overnight to prevent spoilage.

Some states have sanitation regulations restricting the type of containers in which condiments may be served. Only containers that are specifically designed for serving condiments may be used for that purpose. Never attempt to clean an empty bottle and refill it with a condiment.

FLOWERS

Flowers were sold in the markets of classical Athens and Rome. In the time of Nero, flower growing for the Roman luxury trade was a thriving industry. The Emperors were said to have spent a fortune on roses from Paestum to adorn banquet rooms. Roman patricians believed that flowers added elegance to their food; chopped violets were added to salads and stewed roses were served for dessert.

After a dormant period, commercial floriculture was stimulated in the late sixteenth century by the importation of tulips from Turkey to England and western Europe. In the Netherlands, a war of speculation in bulbs, which began in 1634, became so wild that the word "tulipomania" was coined. The boom lasted three years before its collapse, with single bulbs selling for as much as 2,600 guilders.

It was not until the Industrial Revolution, however, that the growing of cut flowers and potted plants for sale became a significant business. Increased urbanization combined with a general rise in living standards resulted in rapid growth of the industry on a per capita basis during the late nineteenth and early twentieth centuries.

In 1907, the appearance of the book *Flower Decoration in the House* greatly influenced the development of what is today the art of flower arranging. The author was Gertrude Jekyll, notable in the gardening world. Soon the idea became widely accepted that flower decorations could be planned and designed in such a way as to heighten the quality of a room. Interior decorators added their specialized knowledge to the practice of this view, and a marked development of ideas concerning more individual arrangements of flowers occurred in the 1930s. After World War II, flower arrangement clubs and societies formed and helped to spread information.

A great variety of materials may be used in flower arranging, including branches, berries, leaves, colorful fruit, and even decorative products of the vegetable garden. Properly dried materials can also be used. The value of an arrangement is found in the shapes, sizes, colors, and textures created by these assorted materials.

In selecting flowers for the table, consider fragrance as well as appearance. Highly scented flowers will conflict with the aroma of the foods and for this reason should not be used. Never use potted plants at the table, as they can attract small mites or bugs.

Proper care of cut flowers will extend their beauty and life. Upon delivery, place cut flowers in tepid water in a cool room or refrigerator. Crush hard-wooded stems slightly so they absorb more water. Split soft stems about one-half inch with a knife or scissors. Soft-leaved flowers like poppies are greatly helped if the tips of the stems are dipped a few seconds in boiling water. Shield the heads and blossoms with paper or cloth. This process also helps to revive wilting flowers and wild flowers. Check arrangements daily for water. Nightly refrigeration will also help extend the life of most floral arrangements.

LIGHTING

It cannot be denied that light has a great effect on our moods. The desired atmosphere can be achieved in the dining room with the aid of various forms of light — fluorescent or incandescent lights, gas lamps, candles, or natural sunlight. Lighting can be used to:

Increase or reduce the impression of space in a room

Influence mood, tempo, and atmosphere

Reveal texture and heighten shape and form

Emphasize and display works of art or food merchandising displays

Provide color, animation, and contrast

Indicate directions and project information

Indicate exit and warning notices

Attract attention, as with an inviting entrance light

Within the facility and associated areas, bright lights should be out of view. Textures and shapes are best emphasized with lighting directed at an acute angle to show the surface in strong relief. Pictures, displays, and other features of interest should be illuminated by directional lighting. When evening dining is in subdued light, the illumination should be concentrated over the tables and service areas.

The flicker of candlelight, for creating mood and intensifying atmosphere, is difficult to reproduce artificially. Candle-lights are often equipped with removable and washable globes and refillable inserts. This type of lighting requires frequent cleaning, at least once a day for proper maintenance.

PERSONAL MISE EN PLACE

All mise en place must be complete before the first guest enters the dining room: tables and chairs in place, napkins folded, clean serviceware in proper position on the tables, side stands stocked, and lighting and temperature adjusted. In addition, be sure to have:

An adequate supply of guest checks in proper number sequence

Two pens or pencils in working order

A clean supply of properly folded side towels

Matches, preferably in-house matches

The dining room and staff are now ready for service.

6
SERVING THE GUEST

SERVICE

There are several meanings of the term *service*. Traditionally the group of dishes composing a given part of a meal was called a service. Service can also signify the utensils necessary to serve a particular part of a meal, such as a tea or wine service. Service in this sense would encompass the whole ensemble of objects used at the table: linens, plates, glasses, silver, and holloware.

The most common sense of the word service, however, refers to the manner of presenting a meal to the guest. There are many styles of service, such as French, Russian, American, English, gueridon, voiture, butler, buffet, counter, and cafeteria. The type of service offered at a restaurant will be determined by the menu; by the skill and training of personnel; by ambience; and, ultimately, by the market the restaurant is trying to reach. No style of service is better than another. Each form of service is designed to meet the specific needs and demands of different circumstances.

French Service

Service a la francaise found its roots in the grand couvert of Louis XIV. The meal was divided into three separate parts or services. The first and second service consisted of the soups, game, and roasts that were listed on the menu. The third service was dessert. As the guests entered the dining room, the first service would have already been set up. Hot items were kept warm on *rechauds* or heating units. After eating all courses planned for a given setting, the guests would leave the table while it was cleaned and reset for the second service.

This custom had some distinct disadvantages. The tables were obviously quite overloaded. Aside from an abundance of food, there were such items as rechauds, centerpieces, flowerbaskets, and candelabra. Despite the use of rechauds, the last items served were generally cold or, at the very least, had lost their freshness. With so many dishes served, most guests limited themselves to one or two items and did not have a chance to sample others. In this way, much food was wasted.

Today a simplified version of the original French service can be found in some classic gourmet and grand luxe restaurants. All food is fully or partially cooked in the kitchen. It is brought to the dining room by the assistant waiter and placed on the gueridon. At the guest's table the food is heated or finished, then plated by the waiter, and finally served by an assistant.

Gueridon and Voiture Service

The gueridon is the most important piece of equipment for proper French service. It is often equipped with a rechaud. The fuel is usually alcohol, bottled butane, or sterno. Gueridon service is very similar to French

51

service, except that all items are fully prepared tableside from the gueridon and immediately plated and served.

Voiture service refers to the practice of plating a pre-prepared entree at the guest's table from a voiture. This entree is the special of the day. The meaning of *voiture* loses something in translation. Defined literally, it means a carriage or car. For use in the dining room, a voiture is generally a decorative cart with a heating unit to maintain the warmth of prepared hot foods. Cold foods can also be served from a voiture.

Russian Service

While Russian service is less showy than French service, it is quicker and no less elegant. Speed replaces show-manship. The main goal of Russian service is to assure the guest fully cooked, hot food served in a swift and tasteful fashion. It is especially expedient for banquets or wherever large numbers of people must be served in a short period of time.

For Russian service, all food is fully cooked, art-fully arranged on platters, and garnished in the kitchen. The platters are brought to the dining room by a waiter and presented to the table. The waiter transfers the food from the platter to the guest's plate by the skillful manipulation of a fork and spoon. The waiter holds the platter in his left hand and serves the food with his right hand, from the left side of the guest. (For more detailed information on Russian service, refer to chapter 10.)

Butler Service

The procedures for Butler service are the same as those for Russian service, except that the guests serve them-selves from the platter held by the waiter.

English Service

As with Russian and Butler service, all food is cooked in the kitchen for English service. However, carving is done in the dining room by the host, who then plates the main item. Next, these plates are passed around the table. All other food is brought out to the dining room and placed on the table; the guests then help themselves family style. Often a member of the service staff may do the carving for the host. Such a person must be skilled at carving and should also have an eye for plating in an attractive and appetizing manner.

American Service

For American service all food is fully cooked and plated in the kitchen by kitchen personnel. A waiter picks up the plated food, carries it to the dining room, and serves it to the guest from the left side, with the left hand.

American service is usually employed in fast turn-over, high volume operations. It can be used in more stylish types of dining operations with procedures vary-ing depending on the service needs. It is frequently used for banquets because large numbers of guests can be handled quickly by a limited number of service personnel.

Buffet Service

The buffet table is like a miniature market place, at-tractively displayed to merchandise the food offered. A buffet is often employed to generate simple, fast service during any meal period when a large number of people must be served in a short amount of time.

Guests generally pay a set price and help them-selves as they pass from one food item to the next along the buffet line. Portion sizes can be controlled and the line kept moving by stationing servers along the buffet to assist guests with plating. A carver is often assigned to serve roasted items such as baked ham, prime rib, or turkey. A reduced number of service personnel are em-ployed on a buffet. The rate of food consumption is high, however, and the greater food expense may outweigh the lower cost of labor.

Counter Service

A fast turnover is the goal of counter service. Patrons are seated and served with a minimum of conversation and movement. Pictures of prepared food items are often displayed on the menu or walls to speed decision making.

A server may have from eight to twenty guests to serve. Little time can be spent walking about, so every-thing must be within reach. The counter should be close to the production area so that orders can be placed, picked up, and served quickly. Rhythm and timing must be established between kitchen personnel and service staff to assure a smooth, trouble-free operation.

Cafeteria Service

Most cafeterias are of the self-service variety, whereby the guest selects his own food and carries it to the table.

Attendants are sometimes used to carry the food tray for the guest. Attendants are generally needed for busing tables, although self-busing is common.

RULES FOR SERVICE

A patron frequents a restaurant to partake of food in an exciting, pleasurable, yet relaxing setting. A skilled waiter, regardless of the type of service offered, must orchestrate the dining experience so that the customer's expectations are gratified. If not, the end result for the server will be no return business and below-average gratuities.

Anticipating the customer's needs and wishes is the key to good service. Be one step ahead. Putting a best foot forward without being overbearing must be gradually learned and can be practiced with each encounter.

Good service must also be consistent and logical. There is no one way to serve a meal. Actually, there are three ways: the correct way, the wrong way, and the only way. The correct way is to adhere to the rules as established by management. The wrong way is to disregard house policy for no obvious reason. The only way is to bend the rules to adjust to unique or unforeseen circumstances. For example, most operations instruct service personnel to clear soiled dishes from the patron's right side; this is the correct way. The wrong way would be to arbitrarily remove the soiled dishes from the left side of the patron. However, if two adjacent guests are leaning toward each other engaged in conversation, the only way to remove the soiled dishes of one of the speakers without disruption is from the left side.

Any prescribed procedure for service should not be taken as gospel. Circumstances will constantly arise demanding that service personnel make instant decisions to alter the customary modus operandi. At first, exceptional situations might prove unnerving, but with experience they will be handled as second nature.

While individual foodservice establishments will establish house rules for service, the following guidelines are generally maintained:

All foods are served from the patron's left side with the waiter's left hand. In French service, house policy may dictate that all food be served from the right side with the right hand.

All beverages are served from the patron's right side with the right hand. Some operations classify soup as a liquid, and therefore a beverage. Hence soup can be served from either the right or left side depending on house policy.

All soiled dishes are removed from the patron's right side with the waiter's right hand except bread and butter plates, which are picked up from the left side.

Never "scrape" dishes in front of the guest.

Serve ladies, older persons, and children first.

All courses should be served in the proper order unless specified or requested by the guest. For example, if three guests are having an appetizer and no soup, and one guest is having soup but no appetizer, the waiter should ask if they would prefer the soup served with the appetizer course.

When serving a table, always walk straight ahead, never backwards.

SERVING THE MEAL

"All the world's a stage,
And all the men and women merely players:
They have their exits and their entrances."
William Shakespeare

Shakespeare's description of the world and its inhabitants holds true for the dining room and its staff. For any successful performance one must know when to enter and exit from the stage — that is, to approach and withdraw from the table. The serving of a full course dinner can be divided into successive segments. These segments can be likened to the scenes in a play, a script telling the server when to enter and exit. The progression of the meal takes the following course:

1. Greeting and seating
2. Cocktail
3. Menu presentation and order taking
4. Wine list presentation and order taking
5. Appetizer
6. Soup
7. Salad
8. Entree and accompaniments
9. Fruit and cheese
10. Dessert
11. After-dinner beverages
12. Tobacco
13. Check

These thirteen scenes can be divided into four acts. In scenes one through four the guests and servers meet and take their assigned positions; food and beverage for the upcoming courses is ordered. In Act I then, the audience is seated, the stage set and characters introduced. The next three scenes constitute Act II. Through the presentation of the appetizer, soup, salad, and accompanying wines, the plot is developed. Act III is made up of a single scene, the serving of the entree. This is the high point, the climax of the play. The five scenes of Act IV — fruit and cheese, dessert, after-dinner beverages, tobacco, and finally the check — bring the meal to a logical conclusion. The excitement generated by the entree is resolved by tastefully winding down the meal.

Through it all, the server is an important player. Often on center stage, he is the common thread holding the play together from scene to scene. His actions set the pace and tempo of the production. In the end, the server's interpretation of his role will determine whether the show will be a comedy, farce, tragedy, or drama. Even so, if the play is a hit he is seldom considered the star; if it is panned, he is generally the scapegoat. Little wonder that in the foodservice industry it is widely known that a good waiter can make up for a poor performance by other restaurant personnel, but that no amount of skill in the kitchen can compensate for a less than polished showing by the waiter. So on with the show!

Greeting and Seating

Guests will be greeted by the maitre d'. A warm smile with good eye contact will help make the reception a success. The appropriate verbal greeting should accompany the smile — "Good morning," "Good afternoon," or "Good evening," as appropriate. Assist guests with wraps, umbrellas, and parcels. Check these items at the appropriate place.

After the reservation has been verified, the guests are seated at the assigned table. It is traditional to seat ladies first. Extra place settings and chairs should be added or removed prior to seating. This gives guests the impression that the table was set just for them. Once all the guests have been comfortably seated, it is time to take the cocktail order.

Cocktail

It is the practice in some operations to serve bouillon to guests before cocktails. Bouillon will coat the stomach and lighten the effects of any alcohol con-

Figure 6.1. Greeting Guests.

Figure 6.2. Assisting Guests with Wraps.

sumed. Being both a food and a liquid, it can be served from either the right or left side. Bouillon is placed directly onto the service plate.

At this point, the assistant waiter may serve rolls. As the bread and butter plate is to the left of the cover, rolls are served from the left. Note the use of the fork and spoon for serving the roll. The same technique is used in Russian service.

Request the cocktail order. If there is a house specialty, be sure to mention it. Then record the cocktail order. Repeat the name of each cocktail as it is ordered. Excuse yourself from the table by stating to the host, keeping eye contact with the entire table, "I will be right back with your order."

Declare each cocktail as you serve it. This will immediately clarify any mix up on the order. Serve the cocktails from the right. Place them to the right of each cover or directly on the service plate. If no service plate has been set, place the cocktail directly in front of the guest.

Figure 6.3. Checking in Wraps.

Figure 6.4. Seating Guests.

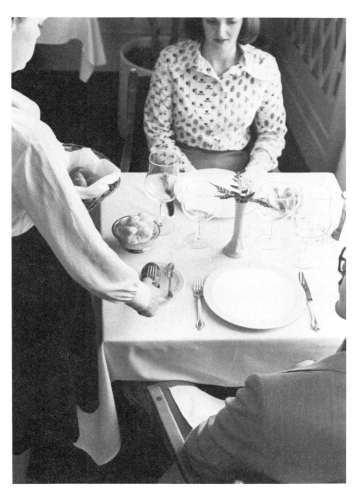

Figure 6.5. Serving Rolls.

Figure 6.6. Taking Cocktail Orders.

Figure 6.7. Serving Cocktails.

Menu Presentation and Order Taking

After the cocktail has been served, the menu is presented to the guests. Serving the cocktail before the menu is presented will encourage a more adventuresome and possibly larger order.

The menu may be presented by either the maitre d', head waiter, captain, or waiter. Present the menu from the left with the left hand whenever possible. If this procedure will be awkward, present the menu in whatever fashion will disturb the guest least. At this time, make the guests aware of any specials that are being promoted during the meal period. Give a full explanation of menu items that might be unclear or foreign to the guests. Be honest without being negative in answering pointed questions such as, "How is the soup today?" This will establish a feeling of trust between guest and server.

Observe the table after a reasonable amount of time passes (five to ten minutes) and ask politely, "Are you ready to order?" If the guests need more time, withdraw and return in a few minutes.

The order is generally taken from the right, but as with all dining room procedures, take the order in whatever manner will disturb the guest least. When requesting the order for a table of two, it is important to establish eye contact to see who will order first. Traditionally, the male will order for the female and then follow with his order. This should not be assumed, however, especially with today's changing social standards. When both guests are of the same sex, the elder is usually first to order, followed by the younger. When there are four or more guests in a party, each one usually orders separately. Start with the guest to the left of the host and work your way clockwise around the table. The host orders last.

Seat numbers are generally assigned by the house to specific places at the table. Order taking throughout the meal should be done with reference to these seat numbers. Regardless of the sequence in which an order is taken, the person seated in chair number two stays number two on the check. Consequently, you can refer to the check to see who gets what food items at service time.

Take each person's complete dinner order at one time. Repeat each item after it is ordered to be sure you are recording the correct selection. Be sure to note on the guest check special requests, timing preferences, and degrees of doneness — for example, "No potato, delay the entree, steak medium-rare." After the order is taken, house policy may dictate the summarization of the order and the use of a dupe (see chapter 9).

Wine List Presentation and Order Taking

After the food order has been taken, the wine list is presented to the host by the sommelier, maitre d', head waiter, captain, or waiter. This is done after the food order because the selection of wine will depend on the choice of food.

Remember, the more special the wine list presentation, the more effective the sale. If only one wine has been ordered, suggest a special wine or a multiwine meal, such as a split of white and a split of red instead of a full bottle of either. This will most certainly enhance the meal by creating a new wine experience for the guests without necessarily increasing the check average. Suggest a light wine for starting the meal, possibly a full-bodied wine for the entree, and, of course, champagne for dessert.

Record all pertinent information concerning the wine order such as name of the wine, bin number, and price. Do not confuse the wine order with the dinner order. Inquire as to when the host wants the wine served.

Figure 6.8. Presenting Menu.

Figure 6.9. Taking Food Order.

Figure 6.10. Presenting Wine List.

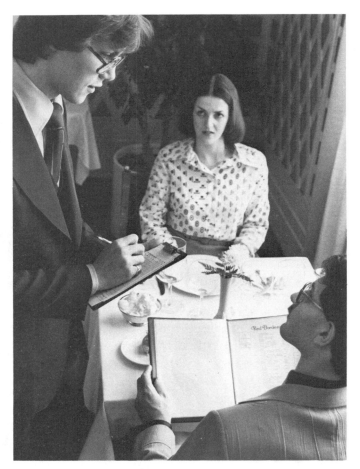

Figure 6.11.   Taking Wine Order.

Figure 6.12.   Setting Appetizer Fork.

Appetizer

Before the appetizer is served, all needed utensils must be set in place. Clean flatware should be carried to the table on a clean dinner plate and napkin by the assistant waiter. The appetizer fork is placed beside the dinner fork. If wine is to accompany the appetizer, it must be served before the food. This is usually done by whoever took the wine order.

After the wine has been poured, serve the appetizer from the left with the left hand. Serve women first. Accompanying sauce may be served by the assistant waiter from the guest's left. Bread and rolls should be checked and, if necessary, replenished at this time.

It is important that premium quality ingredients be used in the production of the appetizer, as this course will establish the tone for the entire meal. A good first impression of the food can successfully offset possible problems later in the meal. When all guests at the table have finished, remove the soiled plates and utensils, as well as anything served to accompany the appetizer.

Figure 6.13.   Presenting Wine.

Figure 6.14. Pouring Host's Wine.

Figure 6.16. Serving Sauce.

Figure 6.15. Serving Appetizer.

Soup

The assistant waiter sets the appropriate soup spoon in place beside the dinner fork. Once this has been done, serve the soup. Soup, even though a liquid, is customarily considered a food item and therefore served from the left. As usual, soiled dishes and flatware are removed from the right.

As appetites become satiated, the waiter must present dishes with flair and style. This will not only keep the patron's interest in the meal keen, but also the server's.

Salad

As explained earlier, greens should be reserved until after the entree. Because greens have a lightening and relaxing effect on the stomach, their consumption after the main course will help prepare the guest for dessert. Also, three courses served prior to the entree

Figure 6.17. Setting Soup Spoon.

Figure 6.19. Setting Salad Flatware.

Figure 6.18. Serving Soup.

Figure 6.20. Serving Salad.

add up to a considerable amount of food. Delaying the service of salad will allow the guest to better appreciate the entree. According to custom, however, most American operations serve salad before the main course.

As with the appetizer and soup courses, all necessary tableware must be set in place prior to the service of the salad. The salad fork is positioned to the left of the dinner fork. If a knife is needed for the salad, it is positioned to the right of the dinner knife. The salad itself is served from the left side of the guest, with the left hand. A pepper mill may be offered or left at the table.

After the completion of the salad, the table must be prepared for the entree. All dishes, flatware, and glassware which were used with the salad should be removed. Generally the cover plate is removed at this time. Many operators, especially those using expensive cover plates, instruct their staff to remove the cover plate even before the appetizer.

Entree

The entree is the high point of the meal. It usually takes more time to be consumed and, for optimum enjoyment, a leisurely air should prevail at the table.

Palates have been appeased and thirsts quenched. The task of rekindling the guest's interest in partaking of yet another course falls on the waiter. Special presentations like sous cloche, en papillote, flambe, and tableside cookery help in this regard. However, a simple but well-designed plate which offers pleasing contrasts in color, texture, and contour, and which is presented by the server with just the right amount of flair and style, is often all that is needed to bring the patron's attention back to the focal point of the meal.

If wine is to accompany the entree, it should be poured at this time. First, the host tastes the wine for approval. Then women are served, followed by the men, and finally the host.

Figure 6.21. Pouring Host's Wine for Approval.

Figure 6.22. Serving Lady's Wine.

The flatware for the entree has already been set prior to the guests' arrival; there should be no need to set it now. However, if the entree calls for any special utensils, such as a lobster pick, position them before the main course is brought into the dining room. If a gueridon is to be used for preparing, finishing, or plating the entree, be sure that it is equipped with all needed serviceware.

Present the entree to the table so the guests can view the platter arrangement. When plating the food move swiftly yet gracefully. Plate the entree first and then any accompaniments such as vegetable and potato. Place the food on the plate in a manner that will facilitate eating and cutting by the guest. The entree item should be placed so that the guest does not have to cut over the accompaniments. Generally, the main course is served with the entree in the lower, center portion of the plate. If accompaniments are served on separate dishes, they are placed on the table after the entree.

House policy may dictate a verbal check of satisfaction by the waiter after the guests have started to eat.

Figure 6.24. Carving Entree.

Figure 6.25. Plating Entree and Accompaniments.

Figure 6.23. Presenting Entree Platter.

Figure 6.26. Serving Entree.

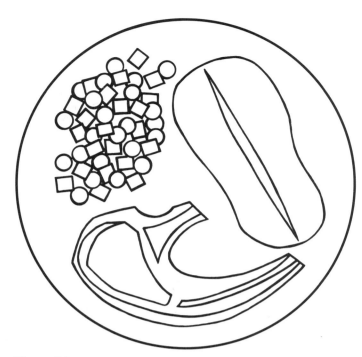

Figure 6.27. Setting Plated Food on the Table so that Entree is Directly in Front of Guest.

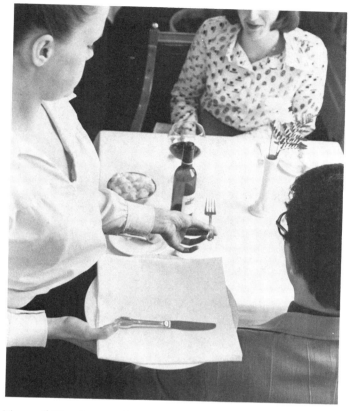

Figure 6.28. Setting Flatware for Cheese and Fruit.

Preferably the presence and awareness of the server will be sufficient to reveal any problems. As the main course progresses, be sure to replenish rolls and bread when necessary, and to repour wine as needed. After the guests have completed the entree, clear the table in the same manner as in the previous courses. Leave the bread and butter plate and knives. These will be used during the next course.

Fruit and Cheese

Fruit and cheese are served together in the United States. In France, purists do not like to mix foods but prefer to serve them *sans melange*, or pure and unblended. Normally, a cheese board of as few as three or four contrasting cheeses is adequate for even the most discriminating diner. A simple cheese course is offered in some establishments along with the salad, especially if a respectable Stilton or Roquefort is available. This simplifies the cheese course, but does it with style. There should also be variety in the accompanying fruit. Be sure that only fresh, ripe fruit is offered. Due to seasonal variations and fluctuating market availability, it is generally a good idea not to specify on the menu exactly which fruit will be served.

Before the cheese and fruit cart is presented to the table, the assistant waiter should set a knife and fork in the appropriate places. Arrange the cart in a neat and organized fashion. Check your mise en place: knives to cut cheese and carve fruit, a bowl of clean water to wash certain fruits, service forks and spoons, plates, and clean napkins.

Allow each guest to make a selection of fruit and cheese. Carefully slice and plate the desired cheeses. Fruits such as grapes will need to be washed. Using a fork to hold a small cluster, dip the grapes into clean water. Place them onto a clean linen napkin on an

Figure 6.29. Presenting Cheese and Fruit Cart.

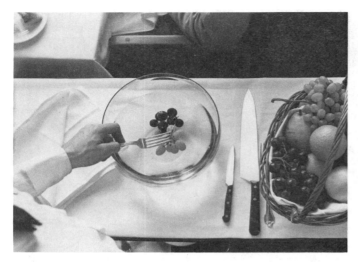

Figure 6.30. Shocking Grapes in Ice Water.

Figure 6.31. Plating Grapes.

Figure 6.32. Fruit and Cheese on Table.

appropriate-sized plate, serving from the left. Much food has been consumed by this time, so keep portions modest — about one-half to one ounce of cheese. If guests desire more after completing their first serving, of course accommodate them.

When the guests have completed the fruit and cheese course, everything which will not be used with dessert should be cleared from the table — salt and pepper, bread and butter plates and knives, bread baskets, butter dishes, wine glasses from previous courses, and any other soiled flatware and dishes.

Before dessert, the table should be crumbed. Crumb from both sides of each guest wherever crumbs are present. A special crumber and brush may be used. An alternate approach is to use a folded linen napkin to brush crumbs onto a six inch plate. However, do not crumb if unnecessary, and do so at other points in the

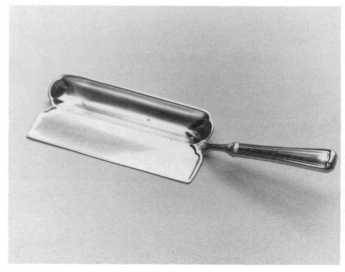

Figure 6.33. Crumber.

Figure 6.34. Crumbing Table.

Figure 6.35. Pouring Champagne.

meal if needed. If a tablecloth becomes soiled during dinner, a half cloth or dinner napkin can be temporarily used to remedy the problem when changing the tablecloth cannot be done with ease.

Dessert

Ending the meal with a superb dessert is as important as beginning it with a quality appetizer. The insatiable sweet tooth of the American public makes dessert a popular course. The profit margin on most desserts makes this sale quite desirable from a management viewpoint.

To increase the chances of selling dessert, sugar in any form — salad dressings, mint jellies for lamb, sweet quick-breads, or sweetened cranberries, etc. — should be eliminated from the dinner menu. A simple and effective approach to merchandising dessert is to exclude it from the menu. The more unique you make the presentation of dessert, or even the idea of dessert, the more effective the sale. Dessert on the menu reminds the guest of the amount of food, both in terms of calories and cost, that he has just consumed. A simple dessert card or separate dessert menu will arouse the patrons' interest and set them up for a sale. A dessert cart which visually stimulates and lures the guest to order is even more effective.

Broussard, a famous restaurant in New Orleans, employs one area of the dining room for the preparation of flaming desserts. This encourages guests to move around and gives the waiter a chance to clean the table. Guests are informed when their desserts are being prepared so they can get up to watch the show.

Figure 6.36. Presenting Dessert Cart.

Figure 6.37. Plating Cake.

Figure 6.38. Serving Dessert.

Before dessert is presented and served, the table must be made ready. Set necessary flatware in place. If the original table setting included dessert flatware above the cover, move them down into the appropriate positions. From the guest's left bring the fork down into position; from the guest's right bring the spoon down. Wine or champagne to accompany dessert should be served at this time.

Before presenting the dessert cart, check to see that all food is appetizingly and neatly arranged. Be sure that the cart is stocked with all necessary serving equipment, including serving forks and spoons, napkins, dessert plates, and clean knives for cutting. A container of warm water may prove useful on the dessert cart. Dipping a knife into warm water before slicing a cake or pie prevents icing from sticking to the knife.

Present the dessert cart and invite the guests to make a selection. Plate each order and serve the dessert from the left side of each guest.

After-Dinner Beverages

Hot beverages such as tea or coffee and after-dinner drinks such as selected cognac, cordials, or after-dinner wine are often enjoyed by guests after a satisfying meal. A wide selection of coffees and teas can be stocked and controlled in the pantry or cold food section of the kitchen. Offering a variety of coffees such as dark roast (espresso), light roast, and even brewed decaffeinated coffee can create menu excitement while satisfying the needs of the patron. A selection of herbal and regular teas, easily stored in boxes or tins, can also be offered to the guest. Liquored hot beverages like Cafe Brulot or Irish Tea can be offered in place of a heavy dessert. This type of selection increases the check average and enhances the completion of the meal.

Before serving after-dinner beverages, deliver all necessary flatware, cups, and accompaniments to the table. Pour coffee at the table from the patron's right side. (For more detailed information on serving coffee and tea, see chapter 7.) Orders for after-dinner drinks are taken in the same manner as before-dinner cocktails. The drinks are served from the right.

Figure 6.39. Serving Coffee.

Figure 6.40.   Serving After-Dinner Drinks.

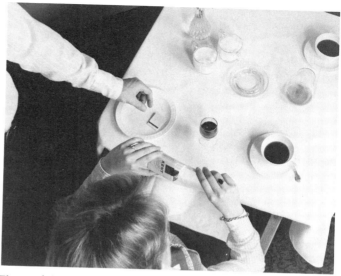

Figure 6.42.   Preparing Matches.

Tobacco

In years past, smoking was traditionally done by men at the completion of the meal. After a meal, men would gather in a room separate from the women with a waiter stationed in attendance at the door.

Figure 6.41.   Presenting Cigarettes and Matches.

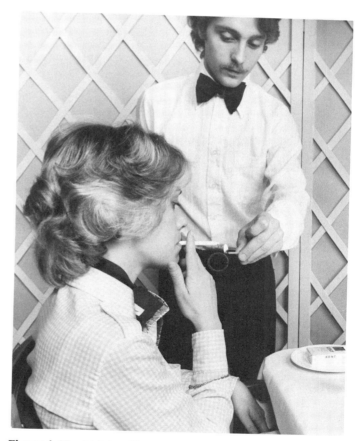

Figure 6.43.   Lighting Cigarette.

With modern ventilation and air purification systems, changing life-styles, and the increase of women smoking, it is now acceptable for both men and women to use tobacco in the dining room. However, more and more health-conscious Americans are protesting public smoking in food establishments, prompting many operators to establish special smoking sections in the dining room. Some local governments have even passed ordinances making separate smoking sections mandatory. In problem areas, air purifiers are recommended to minimize the irritation to nonsmokers.

When cigarettes or cigars are offered and served, an ashtray and a package of matches should be placed to the right of each cover, or one ashtray may be set so as to be conveniently shared by two guests. If a guest requests cigarettes, follow these steps:

Present cigarettes and matches on a small plate.
Reach for the matches as the guest picks up the cigarettes.
Light the cigarette.

Cigar service at the table is usually done from a cart or gueridon equipped with cigars, cedar strips, cigar clipper, ashtray, and matches. Observe this procedure for cigar service:

Present the cigars.
Allow the guest to make a selection.
Unwrap the cigar.
Present the cigar to the guest.
Light the cedar strip.
Light the cigar using the cedar strip.

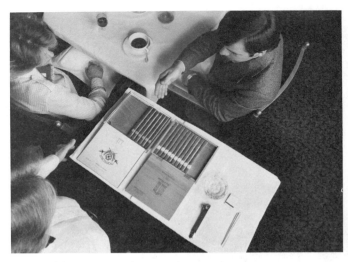

Figure 6.45. Guest Selection of Cigar.

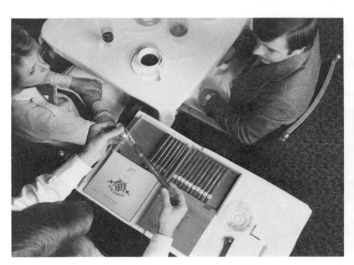

Figure 6.46. Unwrapping Cigar.

Figure 6.44. Presenting Cigars.

Figure 6.47. Presenting Cigar to Guest.

Figure 6.48. Lighting Cedar Strip.

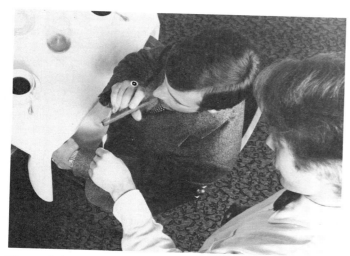

Figure 6.49. Lighting Cigar with Cedar Strip.

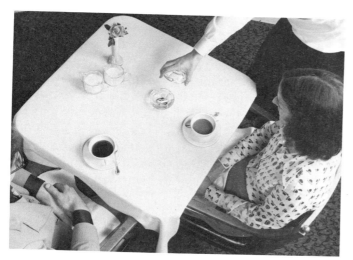

Figure 6.50. Reaching for Soiled Ashtray.

When changing a soiled ashtray, care must be taken to prevent ashes from spotting the tablecloth. Here is one approach:

Reach for the soiled ashtray.
Cap it with a clean ashtray.
Remove both the soiled and clean ashtrays.
Uncap the soiled ashtray.
Return the clean ashtray.

Figure 6.51. Capping Ashtray with a Clean Ashtray.

Figure 6.52. Removing Both Soiled and Clean Ashtrays.

Figure 6.53. Uncapping Soiled Ashtray.

Figure 6.54. Returning Clean Ashtray.

The Check

As the meal nears completion, do not ignore the guests simply because the last course has been served. Make yourself available. Many operations instruct service personnel to present the check only if it is requested by the host. However, if it is obvious that the patrons are waiting for their check, approach the table and ask if any further services are required. The tabulated guest check should be presented in a book or in a simply folded

Figure 6.55. Presenting the Check.

napkin on a dinner plate. The friands ("dainty tidbits") may accompany the check. Like dessert, this *lignappe* (a creole term that means "something extra") is meant literally to leave a sweet taste in the patron's mouth at the completion of the meal.

When picking up the paid check, the waiter stands next to the host, marks the total amount of money received from the guest on the check, and excuses himself. The receipt and any change should be returned in the same manner that the check was presented, either in a book or in a napkin on a plate. (For more detailed information on accepting payment, see chapter 9.)

Be prepared to provide any general information which might be requested, such as other available facilities and services, the location of the restroom and telephones, and suggestions as to entertainment areas in the city.

Assist with the departure of the guests as with their arrival. Help with parcels, wraps, and any personal items left on the table. Bidding the guest farewell should be as engaging as the first hello. Establish a friendly and lasting impression with a sincere manner.

CUSTOMER COMPLAINTS

If a guest seems dissatisfied with the food, beverage, or service, or if the server perceives any potential problem with a guest, it is wise to notify the dining room supervisor or manager. When a food item is returned because it is overcooked, undercooked, or unacceptable in any way, the guest will usually not be charged for a fresh item if the kitchen or dining room is at fault. However, an additional charge should be made if the guest ordered incorrectly in the first place, as when a customer asks that a fresh steak be prepared rare, even though he ordered one well done.

If the guest voices a problem concerning the lighting or the temperature at the table, the waiter should first check to see that the prescribed settings have been accurately maintained. If there is still a problem, the table should be changed to accommodate the guest.

If something is spilled on a guest, first assist the guest and clean up the spill. Of course, an apology is in order. If a serious accident occurs, the dining room supervisor should evaluate the situation immediately and decide if medical attention is required. In the event of any mishap, tending to the guest is of first and foremost importance. Once this has been done, house policy generally dictates the use of an accident report.

This report should include all pertinent information concerning the accident:

> Name of guest
>
> Date and time of accident
>
> Name of server
>
> A complete description of the accident or spill (including photographs of the area, if possible)

It is better to act than to react to a situation. Always stay in control no matter how trying the circumstances. Whenever possible attempt to:

> Listen carefully to the problem.
>
> Apologize for any inconvenience.
>
> Never argue or raise the tone of the conversation.

The finesse demonstrated in handling problems will encourage or discourage the future patronage of each guest present in the dining room.

LOADING, LIFTING, AND CARRYING A TRAY

Many restaurant accidents can be prevented by the correct manipulation of trays in the dining room. Proper balance with equal distribution of items is essential for transporting food and related items. Certain guidelines should be followed in loading a tray to insure safe and sanitary handling.

> If there is not a cork or nonskid surface on the tray, a damp side towel should be placed on the tray to prevent items from slipping.
>
> Place heavy items in the center of the tray and slightly towards the carrier.
>
> Position flatware and smaller items toward the outer edge of tray.
>
> Do not stack cold food on top of hot food if plate covers are used. Heat travels upward and so the cold plate will be warmed.
>
> Liquid carriers (coffee pots, water pitchers) should be placed towards the center of the tray.
>
> Nothing should project over the edge of the tray where it can be easily jarred.
>
> Common china like saucers or cups may be stacked.

Open plates containing food should be held well away from the hair.

Do not overstack or overfill a tray. Get help or make two trips.

Bus boxes are often used in operations with a high turnover rate and where speed is important. When loading a bus box, rest it either on a rolling cart, a tray stand, or the seat of a chair adjacent to the table. Place refuse into one corner of the bus box. Load the largest dishes first. Place heavy items in the center. Items like cups and bowls may be nested. Glasses should be placed upright to one side; do not put anything into glasses which might cause them to tip over. Flatware should go

Figure 6.56. Balanced Tray.

Figure 6.57. Balanced Cocktail Tray.

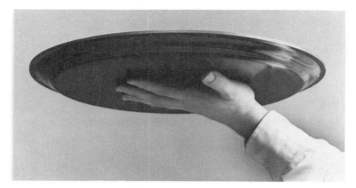

Figure 6.58. Hand Under Tray — Full Palm.

Figure 6.59. Hand Under Tray — Fingertips.

Figure 6.60. Tray Held Waist High.

on the other side. Load butter dishes, creamers, or other food receptacles last. Carry the bus box over the shoulder or in front of the body.

When carrying stacked dishes without using a tray, do not carry more than you can handle. Never rest a stack of plates in the bend of your arm or the stack may collapse. Carry them directly in front of you and hold them slightly away from your body. Practice is essential in developing tray and dish handling skills. Heavy trays and awkward loads should not be attempted until the carrier is confident.

To lift a tray, allow six inches of the tray to project over the edge of the tray stand, side table, shelf, or counter on which the tray is resting. Place the flattened palm under the edge of the tray towards the middle of the broadside. Grip the edge of the tray with the free hand; if the tray is heavy, keep your hand there. Bend carefully at the knees and lift with your legs and back, not your arms, as you slide the tray out and onto your flattened palm. When carrying a tray at shoulder level, known as a "high carry," hold the upper arm close to the body and secure the elbow in position. The tray can be rested on the shoulder for additional support. The high carry is particularly effective when a tray must be carried through a crowd.

Figure 6.61. High Carry.

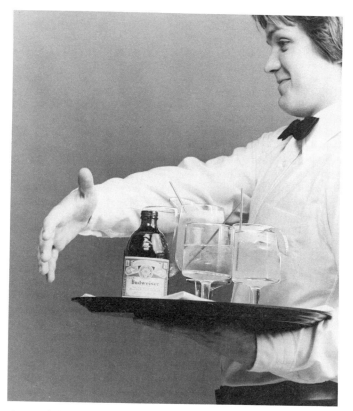

Figure 6.62. Guarding Tray.

Figure 6.64. Carrying Dishes—Wrong Way.

Figure 6.63. Carrying Dishes—Correct Way.

When carrying the tray at waist level, keep the shoulders back. Slouching shoulders will cause the tray to be unstable. The weight of the tray should rest on the hand. While the tray may touch the forearm, the load should not rest there. If the weight rests on the forearm, the tray can be easily tipped. To maneuver through a crowd, guard the tray with the unoccupied hand.

Some people prefer to rest the tray on their spread fingertips instead of their flattened palm. They feel it gives more balance and maneuverability. Only experience can tell what will work best for you. Try both methods and decide for yourself. Practice first with an empty tray. When the empty tray feels comfortable, practice with a loaded tray.

If the doors through which you must pass are hinged on the right, carry the tray in your left hand; if they are hinged on the left, carry the tray in your right hand. This will enable the free hand to open the door and protect or balance the tray. However, if either the right or left hand is not strong enough to support a loaded tray, use the sturdier hand.

The guest should never be served directly from, and the table should never be cleared directly onto, a large tray being held by the waiter. In French service, the table is always cleared by hand, without the use of a tray.

7
BEVERAGE SERVICE

Early man drank for survival; modern man drinks for pleasure. Throughout the years civilization has devised beverages of all kinds to make drinking more gratifying and interesting. We enjoy these inventions today in the form of infusions (tea and coffee), fermented beverages (wine and beer), and distilled beverages (whiskey, brandy, and other spirits).

Aside from being a source of pleasure in their own right, beverages complement food. Dining room personnel must, therefore, be familiar with the patterns of beverage service to orchestrate a pleasurable dining experience for the guest.

WINE

Since wine holds a unique place in dining, it is essential that the dining room professional acquire a basic working knowledge of this special beverage.

Wine is a living beverage made from the naturally fermented juices of grapes. As a living organism, it has a life cycle: it is born; it matures; it may get sick and recover, or die. The living cells in wine are yeast *saccharomyces.*

The head of the vineyard and person in charge of wine-making is the vintner. Under the guidance of the vintner, the vines are cultivated throughout the year. A vine may take five years before producing fruit. These vines may continue being productive for another twenty or so years.

Wine achieves its magical character through the process of fermentation. Fermentation will occur naturally when sugar and yeast meet under the proper conditions. In the process of wine fermentation, the living organism yeast, found on the outside of the skin of ripe grapes, transforms sugar, naturally present in grape juice, into alcohol and carbon dioxide. The carbon dioxide passes off into the air leaving the alcohol in the wine. Specific wines obtain their distinct characteristics partly from the control of the fermentation process.

Vintage

The word "vintage" has several meanings which it would be well to explain.

Vintage means the gathering and pressing of the grapes, and the making of wine therefrom. There is a vintage every year.

The date on a bottle of wine signifies the year in which the wine was produced — the *vintage year.*

Some vineyards bottle and date every year's production; others date only the better years. Certain regions, notably Champagne and Porto, date only the wines of exceptional years. These superior wines are known as *vintage wines*.

A vintage chart can be helpful, but it is important to remember that table wines are living things which are constantly changing. No two wines, even of the same district, are going to develop at a constant rate. Furthermore, not all the wines made in a great year are great, and not all wines made in a relatively poor year are poor. Sweeping generalities of this kind cannot be applied, especially when one considers the thousands of vineyards involved. Vintage charts can be used as a guide to the probable quality of the wine of a given year.

Types of Wines

The four types of wine produced from grapes are:

Table or still: 14 percent or lower alcohol
Sparkling: 14 percent or lower alcohol
Fortified: 18 to 23 percent alcohol
Aromatic: 18 to 20 percent alcohol

Table or still wine is the first level of wine. It is simply grape juice, without any additions, fermented once.

Sparkling wine is produced in three ways:

1. *Champagne:* Fermentation first occurs in vats; then the blended wine is bottled and a "dosage" of yeast and sugar is added to activate a second fermentation in the corked bottle. The dosage produces carbon dioxide which is trapped in the bottle, resulting in sparkling wine. The amount of the dosage affects the sweetness of the wine, as shown in the following table. More sophisticated clientele usually prefer the dryer, less treated wines.

Dosage and Sweetness.

Type	Dosage	Sweetness
Brut	0–1½%	Very, very dry
Extra Sec	1–2%	Extra dry
Sec	2–4%	Dry
Demi Sec	4–6%	Semi dry
Doux	8–10%	Sweet

2. *Charmat.* The Charmat method produces sparkling wines in bulk. While still wine is in its preliminary tank, it is artificially aged by increasing the heat. Once transferred to tank No. 2, it is cooled and sugar and yeast are added for the second fermentation. The third tank is for clarification which is done by refrigerating the wine. Finally, the wine is filtered and bottled.
3. *Soda.* This is the least desirable technique for producing a sparkling wine. The unnatural sparkle is created by gassing the product with carbon dioxide.

Fortified wines are still wines to which brandy has been added to either stop fermentation or increase the alcohol content. Examples of fortified wines are Port, Sherry, and Madeira.

Aromatized or aromatic wines are still wines which undergo complete transformation by the addition of such flavoring agents as sugar syrups, unfermented grape juice, brandy, alcohol, wormwood, hyssop, quinine, juniper, corriander, cloves, camomile, orange peel, and sometimes even rose petals. Sweet and dry vermouth are examples of aromatized wines.

Labels

The wine label is the information card of that specific wine. Every wine bottle contains at least one main label, and some feature neck and back labels with additional information concerning the locale or the company which produces or bottles the wine.

While each wine producing country has its own set of regulations governing the labeling of wines, all wines brought into the U.S. must list the alcoholic content of the wine. The label will also indicate whether the wine is a sparkling or still table wine. Most labels reveal the region and often the vineyard or commune in which the wines were produced. If there is no neck label, the vintage (if there is one) will appear on the main label, together with the name of the producer and/or shipper of the wine, as well as the importer. Any designation or special quality will also be shown.

French labeling is strictly regulated by laws known as *appellation d'origine controlee*, which guarantee that the wine was made in the area named and that its quality is the same as is traditionally associated with that region. The word *chateau* appears on many labels. It literally means the "house" or "villa" which is attached to and owns the vineyard which produced grapes for that specific wine. Wines which are "chateau bottled" or "estate bottled" are wines of better quality and may be labeled *mis en bouteilles au chateau, mis au domaine,* or *mis en bouteilles au domaine.* The word *cru* literally means "growth" in French and generally implies a wine of better or superior quality, with *grand cru* and *premier cru* being even higher designations. The letters V.D.Q.S. stand for *Vins Delimites de Qualite Superieure,* or "delimited wines of superior quality." These are wines from certain regions of France which are good enough to be quality-controlled and exported, but not equal to the caliber of the wines of *appellation d'origine controlee.* V.D.Q.S. stands, in effect, for a secondary classification of the better wines of France.

German wine labels are of three classifications. The first, table wine, in German *Tafelwein,* denotes light, pleasant wines from diverse areas and made from approved grape varieties. In the second category, quality wine, or *Qualitatswein* in German, stands for wines of average quality from a designated area and bearing the name of the vineyard or village. The final classification is quality wine with special attributes, or *Qualitatswein mit Pradikat,* encompassing wines of the highest order which have special qualities. These qualities are also classified by law. The first, *Kabinett,* means that the wine is from fully mature grapes with no sugar added. *Spatlese* means that the grapes are left on the vine past their fully ripe and mature stage to allow them to acquire a higher sugar content, thereby producing a sweeter and more alcoholic wine. *Auslese* indicates that the bunches of grapes have been individually selected for their ripeness and perfect quality, thereby producing a sweeter, more expensive wine. *Beerenauslese* and *Trockenbeerenauslese* are very sweet, very expensive wines whose grapes were individually picked from the bunch by hand when they were very ripe and drying. *Eiswein* is a special type of wine similar to the last two classes. It is made from grapes the water content of which has been frozen by the first frost. The inner concentration of these frozen grapes, rich in sugar and aroma, is squeezed out. These wines are also very expensive and are not always available.

The wines of Italy fall under three labeling classifications: simple, controlled, and controlled and guaranteed. These classifications are regulations for controlling place names, or denomination of origin, much like the French system of appellation d'origine controllee. Simple denomination, *Denominazione de Origine Semplice,* is allowed to ordinary wines made from grapes traditionally cultivated in the area. Controlled denomination, *Denominazione di Origine Contrallata,* usually abbreviated D.O.C., is a classification of wine which has achieved the stipulated standards of quality. Vineyards producing such wines are inscribed in an official register. Controlled and Guaranteed, *Denominazione de Origine Controllata e Garantita,* is the classification awarded only to the fine wines attaining qualities and prices established by recommendation of the Ministry of Agriculture and Forestry.

The wines of the United States are labeled with either generic, varietal, or proprietary names. Generics are those wines which are labeled after broad categories or regions, such as Chablis or Burgundy. Varietal wines are those labeled with the name of the primary grape variety used in making the wine. This can be very misleading, however, because the law states that only 51 percent of the wine need consist of that varietal grape. Forty-nine percent can be comprised of 49 different grape varieties, thereby comprising the true flavor of the grape variety specified on the label. Proprietary names are those brand names adopted by the specific bottler for sales purposes. These names have absolutely no bearing on the wine itself.

Tasting Wine

The tasting of wine utilizes more than the taste buds in the mouth. To appreciate the character of a wine the senses of taste, sight, and smell must be used.

Color and clarity. To determine the color and clarity of a wine, tip the glass and examine the edge of the wine against a white background. Red wines lose color with age and fade from red-purple to ruby to red, red-brown, mahogany, tawny, and finally to amber-brown. White wines develop color with age and change from pale greenish yellow to straw yellow to gold, old gold, yellow-brown, amber-brown, and finally to brown. Rose wines age from pale pink to amber to orange.

Body. To judge the body of the wine, swirl the glass and notice the drippings or legs running down the side of the glass from the rim. A dry light wine will have thin legs that flow quickly; a heavy bodied wine will have slower, thicker legs.

Aroma. Two thirds of the judgment of a wine are formed from the aroma. To release the bouquet, swirl the wine and let it evaporate against the side of the glass. With more surface in contact with the air, the bouquet is intensified. An attractive, fruity aroma is characteristic of young wine. A flowery aroma is found in many light wines. The big red wines need five to ten minutes in a glass to fully develop their bouquet. Unpleasant odors indicate an unpalatable wine.

Taste. Take a little wine in the mouth. "Whistle" in the wine, and actually chew the wine to expose it to all the taste buds. The front of the tongue will determine sweetness, the back bitterness, and the sides sourness and saltiness. Judge the wine for degree of sweetness, acidity, and tannin. Excessive acidity is unpleasantly tart, too little is dull, but balanced acidity gives a pleasant, lively sensation. Tannin in a young red wine shows up in a puckerish quality which will diminish as the wine gains balance with age. Tannin is essential for proper development of any good red wine.

Dining room personnel not only serve wine; they also sell wine. Keep in mind that the customer's impression of a wine, as well as other parts of the meal, is influenced not only by how the wine tastes, but also by the manner in which the wine is presented, opened and served. Try to taste several wines of the same general character at one time to develop your judgment and experience. Keep a notebook to help you remember wines previously tasted. You need only record the name, vintage year, the producer, the cost, and very brief comments. Many restaurants will make provisions for sales personnel to taste the wines being offered on the wine list.

Wine Storage

For a wine to be at its best when opened, it must be stored properly. The higher the alcoholic content of a wine, the longer it can be stored and the easier it is to transport. Some serious enemies of wine are contact with air, extreme heat or cold, fluctuations in temperature, vibration, sunlight, and odors.

Store wine in a dark, well-ventilated, insulated, and temperature-controlled room. Storage temperature for all wine is between 55°F and 60°F (12.8°C to 15.6°C). Always keep the wine stored at a constant temperature. Juggling the temperature can result in the death of the wine.

Wine bins must be sturdy and wine bottles secured against rolling. This is especially important with robust red wines where sediment is inevitable with age. Store wines horizontally. This will keep the cork moist and prevent it from shrinking. A shrunken cork allows air into the bottle, which spoils the wine.

Face wine labels up so that the wine can be identified without moving the bottle. Identify the bins with numbers and/or labels. Some restaurants use small numbered labels on top of the bottle corresponding to numbers designated for the wine on the wine list. This allows for fast identification without touching the bottles.

Figure 7.1. Wine Cellar "21" Club, New York City.

Figure 7.2. Personalized Wine Bins at "21" Club, New York City.

Convenient access to the wine room from the dining area is essential; otherwise a forward or par stock in the dining room is advisable. This par stock may be kept at the bar, in a wine display, or in a storage cabinet somewhere in the dining room. If possible, provide refrigeration for the par stock of whites and roses, and forward bin space for the faster-moving reds. In a growing number of restaurants, the bartender holds a small supply of popular white wines under refrigeration and the waiter pulls an unchilled bottle to trade with the bar for a chilled one. In this way, the bar's chilled stock remains constant.

Always rest wines a few days after receiving. Remember that the smaller the bottle, the faster the wine will mature. Wine will mature more quickly in a warm room, although this is an undesirable practice.

Wine Serving Aids

For the patron to fully enjoy and appreciate wine as part of the dining experience, all wine service equipment must be handled properly. For service to proceed smoothly, wine coolers and decanters, napkins, candles, corkscrews, and baskets must be ready for use at all times. Mise en place is extremely important — in the dining room as well as in the kitchen.

Corkscrews. There are many varieties of corkscrews on the market. The traditional T-type is rather difficult to use without disturbing any sediment present in the bottle. Inexperienced waiters and many consumers will find the butterfly or double screw types easier to use, but most professional wine waiters prefer the lever type corkscrew, which folds to a convenient pocket size. This is also known as a "waiter's" corkscrew. The best corkscrew is generally conceded to have a hollow spiral

Figure 7.3. Coded Wine Tags, Escoffier Room, Hyde Park, New York City.

Figure 7.4. Wine Rack with Refrigerated Section for White and Rose Wine, Escoffier Room, Hyde Park, New York.

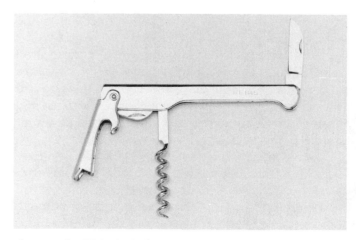

Figure 7.5. Waiter's Corkscrew.

Figure 7.6. Assorted Corkscrews.

worm with the point in a direct line with the spiral. The outside of the spiral may be grooved, which gives a stronger grip on the cork. The spiral should be long enough to penetrate to the bottom of a two inch cork.

Wine buckets. Whatever its style, a wine bucket has one simple purpose: to chill wines. To do this effectively, fill the bucket three-quarters full of ice and water. The water makes it easier to place the bottle deep into the ice for quick, thorough chilling. Napkins should be draped on the wine bucket for service.

Wine baskets. Wine baskets are only used with red wines. Their primary function is to make possible the gentle transfer of a mature red wine from cellar to table. Some restaurants serve all red wines from baskets; others simply stand a young red on the table.

Figure 7.7. Wine Bucket with Stand.

Figure 7.8. Wine Basket.

Glassware for Wine Service

There are almost as many types of wine glasses in existence as there are wine regions. In Switzerland, Swiss wines are served in small straight-sided tumblers similar to our fruit juice glasses. In Greece, all local wines are served in small old-fashioned glasses. Both countries, however, serve imported wines in stem glasses. A large restaurant or hotel may have a half dozen or more different sizes and shapes of glasses, but the moderate-sized restaurant can get along very well with one all-purpose wine glass. This can be a clear, tulip-shaped glass with a capacity of about 8 oz, but of course it should never be more than half full.

If more than one all-purpose glass is desired, consider both the size and shape in making a selection. The size of the glass must be compatible with the table setting, yet large enough to allow for a generous serving of wine to be swirled. Aperitif and dessert wine glasses generally have a 4 or 5 oz capacity. Red wine glasses will have a capacity of from 9 to 12 oz. If a red wine glass is any larger, the wine can loose its bouquet and aroma. White wine glasses, with a capacity of from 7 to 9 oz, are generally smaller than red wine glasses. Since white wine is served chilled, a smaller serving is poured, allowing the remainder to stay in the cooler.

The best design for a wine glass is a stable-based, stemmed, bowl-shaped glass with the rim turned in slightly. The white wine glass is tall and the bowl has a smaller opening to capture and hold the aroma and bouquet; the red wine glass has a wider opening to promote oxidation and to release acidity. The stem of the glass must be long enough to permit grasping the glass comfortably without touching the bowl, as this would cause the temperature of the wine to change. A stable base reduces the possibility of tipping the glass. The traditional saucer-shaped champagne glass (tradition says it was originally fashioned after Marie Antoinette's breast) has lost favor. Today it is rapidly being replaced by a tall, narrow, tulip-shaped glass with a 6 oz capacity. This glass is filled to about three-quarters full. The tulip shape enables the champagne to stay cooler longer, allows for the appreciation of the color, and preserves the effervescence. The coupe and hollow-stemmed saucer glass tends to warm the champagne faster and to expel the effervescence more quickly. For this reason it is no longer recommended.

The sight, smell, body, and flavor of a wine are ideally displayed and enhanced in a classic crystal wine glass, as thin as is affordable. Colored glasses were needed in the past to cover sediment and impurities floating in the wine, but today wine glasses should always be clear.

Figure 7.9. White Wine Glasses.

Figure 7.10. Red Wine Glasses.

Figure 7.11. Champagne Glasses. Left to Right: Tulip, Short Fluted, Saucer, Tulip, and Tall Fluted.

Figure 7.12. Holding Wine Glasses. Each glass is held underneath the preceding glasses. Release the glasses in reverse order.

Step a. Hold the base of the first glass between the index and middle fingers.

Step b. Slide the base of the second glass under the first and hold it between the pinkie and ring finger.

Step c. Slide the base of the third glass under the preceding glasses and hold it between the middle and ring fingers.

Step d. The base of the fourth glass is held between the thumb and index finger.

Step e. The base of the fifth glass is held between the index and middle fingers.

Step f. The base of the sixth glass is held in front of the first glass between the pinkie and ring finger.

Figure 7.13. Decanters.

Because the aroma and taste of wine is easily affected by foreign elements, special care must be taken in the washing and storage of glasses. The most effective method for preparing glasses for table is steaming and polishing, then drying with a clean dry cloth. Strong detergents and improper rinsing may leave a residue that will mask the quality of the wine and kill the effervescence in a sparkling wine. Steaming involves no foreign elements like soap to affect the taste. Steaming glasses is a simple procedure. Fill a hotel pan or similar container two-thirds full of water and add a small amount of vinegar. The vinegar will help to eliminate residue and, if the right amount is used, will not impart any taste to the glass. Cover the hotel pan with aluminum foil and make a hole to allow steam to escape. Hold the wine glass by the stem with the bowl directly over the hole, thus allowing the steam to fill the bowl of the glass. Wipe with a clean cloth.

Storage of the glasses is equally important, as all efforts to clean the glasses will be in vain if the storage method soils the glasses. Store glasses upright. If they are placed upside down, they may acquire the smell of anything on which they are resting. If hung from overhead racks, oily smoke and odors can collect on the glass and impair the flavor of the wine. To keep dust or dirt out of the upright glasses, cover them with paper or a clean cloth.

Wine glasses are fragile and expensive, and so, in addition to proper cleaning and storage, they must be handled and carried correctly. Never claw or put your fingers inside of the bowl. Skin oils can only be removed with detergents which, as mentioned, are far from ideal for glasses. Soiled glasses should be handled by the stem or with two fingers around the base of the bowl. Avoid contact with the bowl of the glass at all times.

Handle clean glasses individually, using two fingers and the thumb to hold the stem of the glass. Wine glasses should be placed on the table prior to service as part of the table setting, to help merchandise more wine. If not included in the table setting, they should be stored at side stands or the bar, and be conveniently accessible to the table. After a glass has been polished, the less it is handled, the more attractive it will remain. Transport wine glasses on trays. If a number of glasses are carried by hand, hold them upside down by placing the glasses between the fingers and locking the bases together with the thumb.

Wine decanters are cleaned and maintained in the same manner as wine glasses. As decanters will generally be used for older, more delicate, and more expensive wines, particular care in cleaning, storing, and handling is essential.

Taking the Wine Order

The position of sommelier or wine steward in today's restaurants is rare indeed. It is nevertheless a branch of the culinary arts which should not be too readily set aside. People everywhere are becoming much more aware of wine and its complimentary status with food and entertainment. The fine service of wine may enlighten the guest's knowledge and enhance the occasion, as well as bring back return business.

Whether carried out by a sommelier or a waiter, the wine order should be taken with elegance and grace.

Figure 7.14. Sommelier's Chain with Tasting Cup.

When approaching a table, rest the wine list on the right hand, not under the arm, and present the list to the entire table unless a specific host has been designated earlier. If the menu is special, the wine order will have already been taken in advance. Always be polite and address everyone at the table: "Good evening ladies and gentlemen, would you care to see our wine list?" It can no longer be assumed that one of the gentlemen at the table will ask for the wine list. Any of the guests might make the decision, but it is usually that person who is the host or hostess to whom you will present the wine list. Position yourself to the right of the host or hostess and present the list. If it is a singlefold wine list, present it opened; if it is a multipaged list, present it closed. Quietly excuse yourself and tend to other duties for a few minutes, being watchful of the table. When the host or hostess is ready to order or wishes your assistance, you will know immediately. If the guest wishes to make a selection, do not make any suggestions but merely answer any questions and take the order. However, if the guest desires some assistance in selecting the wine, make an intelligent suggestion based on what the table will be eating for appetizer and/or entree, and the preferences of the guests, such as "not too dry."

Wine charts are used in several restaurants to inform the service staff of which wines are available and what these wines best accompany. These charts allow the staff to make intelligent suggestions to their guests. A typical chart would include the list number (where the wine appears on the wine list), name, phonetic pronunciation, year, bottle size, price, type (red, white, sparkling), origin, serving temperature, characteristics, and recommended accompanying dishes. The more involved charts also deal with the body, flavor, and bouquet. If the personnel are not tasters of wine, however, these words can easily be twisted and misrepresented. Any mention on the wine chart of flavor, body, or bouquet should be simplified to light, medium, medium-dry, dry, sweet. Too much detail will confuse the service personnel and the results may be unfavorable. Wine charts are usually posted in the wine distribution center in the restaurant for easy access and convenience to persons selling this beverage.

If the guest questions how much wine to order, the standard guidelines are: 1/2 bottle (tenth or medium) for two persons; full bottle (fifth or regular) for three to six persons; magnum or two full bottles for seven to twelve persons. The order is then left to the discretion of the host.

When taking the wine order, write everything down — size of bottle, year, type, name, and location code number. The wine list is then removed from the table and the host asked when the wine is to be served. Precise instructions are necessary. If the guest asks that the wine be served with the meal, inquire further to determine with which course it is to be served. Thank the guest for the order and excuse yourself.

Serving Wine

Once the wine has been ordered, a decision must be made as to when it will be opened and served. If the host has given no instruction in this regard, follow these guidelines: white and rose wines are opened and served with the first course, unless requested with the entree; red wines are opened at table and held at room temperature immediately following the presentation to the host. Red wines should be left open as long as possible, ideally one hour before serving. This process of oxidation allows the wine to breathe. After oxidation, serve the red wine just prior to delivering the entree to the table.

If separate wines are to be served for different courses, and if the glasses are to be set for each service, carry the glasses to the table by hand, holding them by the stem, or on a hand tray, or on a wine cart. From the right side of the guest, using the right hand, place the new glass on the table to the left of the previous glass. Then remove the previous glass. If wine still remains in the old glass and the guest wishes to keep it, do not remove it. Glasses should be removed as soon as the previous wine is finished, unless a guest indicates otherwise. In some cases, as at the end of a course or when a wine change has been ordered, it is proper to remove the old glasses regardless of whether or not there is wine remaining.

Make sure the wine is at the proper temperature before serving:

> White: 45°F to 55°F (7.2°C to 12.8°C)
>   Ideal: 48°F (8.9°C)
> Red: 60°F to 75°F (15.6°C to 23.9°C)
>   Ideal: 68°F (20°C)
> Rose: 45°F to 55°F (7.2°C to 12.8°C)
>   Ideal: 45°F (7.2°C)
> Champagne: 38°F to 42°F (3.3°C to 5.5°C)
>   Ideal: 40°F (4.4°C)

These temperature suggestions can be further refined: for reds, the younger the wine, the lower the temperature; the older the wine, the higher the temperature. White and full-bodied sweet wines are served cooler than delicate light ones. Beaujolais is sometimes served cool. Of course, no wine should ever be heated. Allow the wine to arrive at the desired temperature naturally.

Serving Red Wine

Follow these steps when serving red wine:

1. From the right side, present the bottle to the host for approval. If approved, proceed; if not approved, make proper corrections.
2. Open wine at the table or at a gueridon alongside the table (see *Opening Wine*, pp. 85–88).
3. Decant wine if necessary.
4. Pour enough wine — one ounce — into the host's glass for tasting. Face the label out when pouring, to facilitate guests' viewing the label. Twist the bottle at the conclusion of pouring so that the label faces the host. This twisting action will also prevent wine from dripping down the side of the bottle.
5. Place wine in center of table to oxidize.
6. Serve the wine to the guests clockwise around the table. Traditionally, women are served first and then men. If a more informal attitude or style prevails, serve the guests clockwise as they are seated. Fill glasses to about one-third full, or two to three ounces. Hold the bottle so that each guest can view the label as the wine is being served. The host is served last.
7. Distribute the wine evenly to all guests. Replenish wine glasses often. No glass should ever remain empty as long as there is wine in the bottle.
8. Leave the wine bottle on the table until guests depart or a new wine is served.
9. Never completely empty a bottle for fear of pouring out sediment.
10. Suggest a second bottle.

Sediment and Decanting

All wines may develop sediment in the normal process of aging. White wine sediment is usually colorless and does not affect the taste or quality of the wine. The sediment may derive from pectins or tartars and usually disappears in a warm room. If not, stand the bottle upright to allow the sediment to fall to the bottom of the bottle. Decanting is not necessary.

The sediment in red wine comes from tannins or color pigments. Because this sediment has an unpleasant and bitter taste, it should never be allowed into a guest's glass. Decanting is done to draw off the clear wine and to leave any sediment in the bottle.

Ideally, decant the wine as early as possible before it is to be served. This will allow the wine to oxidize and breathe. Contact with air expands the bouquet and enhances the flavor of a wine. Decant as soon as the bottle has been opened.

As mentioned earlier, all wines should be binned with the label up. However, if a wine with sediment has been rested with the label on one side, place it in the basket that way to avoid stirring the sediment. Your knowledgeable wine drinker will appreciate your explanation.

In decanting, be sure to observe the following procedures:

1. Use only a perfectly clean and dry decanter.
2. Move the bottle gently and carefully; preferably have it in a basket.
3. Cut the foil by turning the blade of the corkscrew and not the bottle. Remove all foil from the neck of the bottle.
4. Hold the clear neck of the bottle over a lit candle and pour a few drops of wine into the decanter. Swirl and pour off this bit of wine into an extra glass. This is to insure that nothing in the decanter will contaminate the taste of the wine. Meanwhile, be sure to hold the bottle of wine steadily over the candle.
5. Continue to pour the rest of the wine into the decanter.
6. Closely observe the neck of the bottle and stop pouring the moment sediment appears.
7. Allow the host to taste the wine and, upon approval, inquire as to when the wine is to be served.
8. Serve as usual. The empty bottle remains on the table along with the decanted wine.

White and Rose Wines

White and rose wines must be chilled before serving. As mentioned earlier, the temperature range for serving these wines is from 45°F to 55°F (7.2°C to 12.8°C). Overchilling will reduce the bouquet of the wine.

Fill the wine bucket three quarters full with ice and water. Fifteen minutes in a cooler will sufficiently chill a white or rose wine. Follow these steps when serving a white or rose wine:

1. Position a wine bucket to the right of the host.
2. From the right side, present the wine to the host for approval.

Figure 7.15. Holding Chilled White Wine Bottle.

Figure 7.16. Opening Wine.

Step a. Present the bottle to the host for approval.

3. Place the wine into the wine bucket.
4. Open the wine.
5. Pour enough wine into the host's glass for tasting.
6. Distribute and serve like red wine, except that white and rose wines are kept in the cooler instead of on the table.

When serving a chilled wine, be sure to wipe the water from the outside of the chilled bottle each time the wine is poured. Hold the chilled bottle with a napkin between your hand and the bottle. This prevents your hand from raising the temperature of the chilled wine.

Opening Wine

The following procedure for opening wine calls for the use of a waiter's corkscrew. To open a bottle of wine:

1. Cut foil below lip of the bottle.
2. Remove foil.
3. Wipe mouth of bottle.
4. Push cork down slightly with fingers to break seal between cork and bottle.
5. Insert corkscrew at a slight angle and straighten it up with one powerful turn.

Step b. Cut foil below lip of the bottle.

Step c. Remove foil.

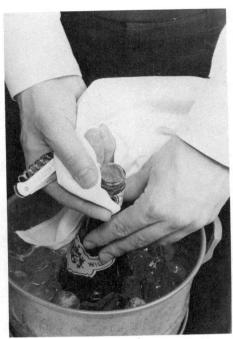

Step d. Wipe mouth of bottle.

Step e. Push cork down slightly with fingers to break seal between cork and bottle.

Step f. Insert corkscrew at a slight angle and straighten it up with one powerful turn.

Step g. Turn corkscrew until only two notches of the spiral are left outside the cork.

Step h. Place lever of the corkscrew on the lip of the bottle.

Step i. Holding the corkscrew in place with the left hand, pull corkscrew straight up, loosening the cork. Do not bend the cork.

Step j. Release lever and turn corkscrew final two notches.

Step k. Continue to lift cork.

Step l. Pull the cork out slowly, without a "pop."

Step m. Smell the cork for any vinegar, sulphur, or musty odor. (If there is any off-smell, bring another bottle at once. Do not be embarrassed — unless you have forgotten to check.)

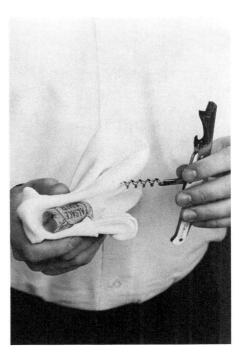

Step n. Remove cork from corkscrew and place it to the right of the host's glass.

Step o. Wipe lip and mouth of the bottle.

Step p. Pour a sample of the wine for the host to taste.

Step q. Twist the bottle as you finish pouring to prevent wine from dripping down the bottle.

6. Turn corkscrew until only two notches of the spiral are left outside the cork.

7. Place lever of the corkscrew on the lip of the bottle.

8. Holding the corkscrew in place with the left hand, pull corkscrew straight up, loosening the cork. Do not bend the cork.

9. Release lever and turn corkscrew final two notches.

10. Pull the cork out slowly, without a "pop."

11. Smell the cork for any vinegar, sulphur, or musty odor. (If there is an off-smell, bring another bottle at once. Do not be embarrassed — unless you have forgotten to check.)

12. Remove cork from corkscrew and place it to the right of the host's glass.

13. Wipe lip and mouth of bottle.

Champagne Service

To serve champagne properly, use the following procedure:

1. Chill in a wine bucket a half hour before serving. More time is required to chill champagne than white wine because the glass of the bottle is thicker.

2. Cut foil capsule below wire and remove.

3. Untwist wire with right hand, holding left thumb on top of the cork.

4. If cork starts to rise, place napkin over the cork; tilt the bottle to a 45° angle; hold the cork in; and allow pressure to escape slowly. This may occur with insufficient chilling.

5. Remove wire and wrap napkin around the bottle. Then hold the cork with left hand, hold the bottle at a 45° angle, and turn the bottom of the bottle with right hand. Hold the cork in to allow pressure to escape slowly. Never allow the cork to pop or escape. Tilting the bottle at a 45° angle for a few seconds after the cork is removed will prevent overflow.

6. Once the cork is removed, wipe the bottle and serve the host for approval. Expose the label when pouring. A napkin may or may not be used.

7. Pour slowly, about three ounces to each guest as with other wines.

8. Return champagne to wine bucket.

DISTILLED SPIRITS

The process of distilling spirits is simple but delicate. Alcohol vaporizes at 176°F. The application of heat to a liquid containing alcohol liberates the alcohol from the original liquid in the form of vapor. This is collected and condensed into raw alcohol, and the temperature is then lowered. This process, when repeated, extracts impurities and increases the proof. Alcohol is chemically pure at 200 proof. Neutral spirits are those which are distilled to a minimum of 190 proof, and at this point are odorless, colorless, and flavorless. Once the process of distillation was discovered, it became inevitable that cultures would use those products closest at hand and in greatest abundance for producing spirits.

Brandy. The ancient art of distillation was not applied commercially until the sixteenth century, when brandy was introduced. Legend tells us of a vigorous trade between the port of La Rochelle on the Charente River and Holland. Due to the perils of war, shipping space was at a premium. An enterprising Dutch shipmaster attempted to condense his wine by distilling it and eliminating the water. He would then transport the soul or spirit of the wine to Holland, where the water would be replaced. After tasting the condensed wine (burnt wine, or *brandewyn*), he decided that he liked it just as it was.

Today brandy is distilled from fruit, grapes being the most popular. Cognac is a type of brandy, but not all brandies are cognacs. Only brandy from the French district of Cognac may bear that district's name. The most distinctive characteristic of a cognac is the magnificent aroma which it imparts when heated in the traditional snifter, either with the hands or with an alcohol flame.

Whiskey. Whiskey comes from the Celtic word *Uisgebaugh* (whis-geh-baw), which means water of life. All whiskey is distilled from grain. There are five types of whiskeys:

1. Scotch: made from barley
2. Bourbon: made from corn
3. Rye: made from rye
4. Canadian: made from cereal grains
5. Irish: made from barley, corn, or rye

Gin. A neutral spirit flavored with the juniper berry, gin was used heavily in England during the reign of Queen Ann (1702-1714) to mask the unpleasant flavor of seventeenth century spirits. *Holland gin* is low in

Figure 7.17. Brandy Glasses. Left to Right: Brandy Snifter, Brandy Snifter, Brandy Sipper.

Figure 7.18. Brandy Snifter Over Alcohol Burner.

proof with a clean and malty aroma and flavor. It should not be mixed with other ingredients to make cocktails, because its own taste will not blend well with other ingredients. *American dry gin* is different in character from Dutch and English gins. Distillers are required under U.S. regulations to use neutral spirits of 190 proof or more. By definition, these spirits do not have any character and are flavored with botanicals. For *English dry gin*, the grain formula is 75 percent corn, 15 percent barley malt, and 10 percent other, distilled to 180 proof and flavored with botanicals.

Rum. Rum is any alcoholic distillate from the fermented juices of sugar cane, distilled at 190 proof and reduced to no less than 80 proof.

Vodka. Vodka was originally produced in Eastern Europe from the most plentiful and least expensive materials available to the distiller. Potatoes, corn, and wheat are the main ingredients. Vodka is distilled at or above 190 proof and reduced to between 80 and 110 proof. It must be rectified through or with vegetable charcoal for at least eight hours. Vodka is not flavored or aged. It is always drunk ice-cold in rather small glasses, and is usually acceptable to be taken with food, such as appetizers.

Tequilla. Tequilla is distilled from a variety of cacti (*genus amaryllis*) near the town of Tequilla, Mexico, northwest of Guadalajara in the state of Jalisco. When produced elsewhere, it is labeled Mezcal.

Cordials and Liqueurs. Cordials and liqueurs are alcoholic beverages flavored with aromatics and usually sweetened.

Figure 7.20. Bar Glasses.

Figure 7.21. Bar Glasses. Left to Right: Cocktail Glass, Cocktail Glass, Footed Rocks Glass, Footed Rocks Glass, Whiskey Sour Glass, Queen-Sized Cocktail Glass.

Figure 7.19. Sweet Wine Glasses.

Making Drinks for Table Service

Bartenders are never to begin any drink until they receive from the waiter both the order, written on an order pad, and a receipt from the precheck machine. This receipt is verification that the order has been entered onto the guest check. The slip from the order pad and the receipt from the precheck machine are stapled together and kept out of reach from all except the bartender.

Figure 7.22. Bar Glasses. Left to Right: Highball Glass, Rocks Glass, Highball Glass, Highball Glass.

Figure 7.23. Specialty Bar Glasses.

Figure 7.24. Specialty Bar Glasses.

Figure 7.25. Bar Tools. Bottom Row (left to right): Ice Tongs, Muddler, Three Pouring Caps, Ice Scoop. Second Row: Cutting Board and Knife, Three Jiggers, Citrus Squeezer. Third Row: Two Mixing Spoons, Pouring Strainer, Citrus Squeezer. Top Row: Cocktail Shaker and Mixing Glass.

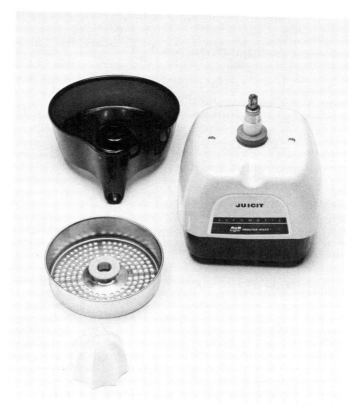

Figure 7.26. Juicer.

Figure 7.27. Electric Mixer, Electric Blender, and Manual Mixer.

All drinks taken from the bar must be carried on a bar tray.

Never substitute one brand for another. If a guest orders a specific brand which is not carried or is out of stock, bring this to the guest's attention and ask if they would care to make another selection.

Mix drinks, such as Scotch and soda, in front of the guest at the tableside. The waiter picks up the proper glass containing ice, a stirrer, an opened split of the appropriate mixer, and the requested brand of liquor poured either into a jigger glass or a two ounce decanter. At the table, the waiter asks if the guest would like the drink mixed. If yes, the waiter pours the liquor into the glass, then pours the mixer until the combined liquid fills half the glass. The drink, along with the remaining soda, is served to the right side of the guest. The same procedure is followed when the drink is ordered with water.

Making Drinks
at Bar, in Front of Guests

Follow these steps when making drinks in the presence of the guests:

1. Greet guests appropriately, always with a smile and offering your services.
2. Obtain order from customer.
3. Write down order on check. Put barstool number in corner of check and circle it.
4. Leave check face up near guest.
5. Prepare the drink. Do not conceal the label of the bottle, and pour directly in front of guests, on top of bar in well.
6. Serve drink with cocktail napkin placed under the glass.
7. Pick up check.
8. Register price on check.
9. Return check to customer.
10. Check for ashtray and peanuts.

Closing Out Checks

A clear sequence should always be followed when closing out checks:

1. Register tax and total on check.
2. Return check to customer and state combined total to the guest.
3. Collect payment from customer. State clearly the total of the check and the denomination

of the money received from the customer; for example, "$10.50 out of $20.00."

4. Register receipt of cash.
5. Deposit paid check in locked box.
6. Return change and count back to guest. "Sir, $10.50 out of $20; Ten fifty, fifty equals eleven, twelve, thirteen, fourteen, fifteen, and five makes twenty. Thank you very much Sir, enjoy your dinner."
7. Clear area where guests were seated.

Duties of Opening Bartender

The bartender who opens the bar should follow these steps:

1. Acquire keys and a Standard Bar Manual.
2. Check to see if there is any function which might require a special spirit beverage or wine not in regular stock, or a function which might call for more than the established par stock for that item.
3. Set up bar according to check list found in the *Standard Drink and Procedure Manual.*
4. The bartender should take requisition and empty bottles to Manager for replacement.
5. Check the register to make sure it has been properly cleared from previous day.
6. Requisitioned items received should be checked by the bartender before putting them away. Wines and beer should be put in their appropriate place in the cooler.
7. During the work period, if business is slow, the bartender should make sure that enough garnishes and fresh dishes are prepared for the next shift.
8. All bar glassware should be washed at the bar; bar glassware is not to go into the kitchen unless requested by management.

Duties of the Closing Bartender

The bartender who closes the bar should follow these steps:

1. Check to see if there is a function which might require a special spirit beverage or wine not in regular stock, or if there is a demand for an item in excess of the established par for it.

2. Set up bar according to check list found in the *Standard Drink and Procedure Manual.*

3. Check to make sure that the cash register has been cleared from the previous shift and that there are no checks which have not been closed out and turned in.

4. All bar glasses must be washed at the bar.

5. At times during the work period when business is slack, the bartender should make sure that there are adequate garnishes prepared for the AM shift.

6. The register should be cleared in the presence of the bartender and maitre d' in charge.

7. All spirits and wines are to be locked up and the bar left in good order before leaving.

8. Make requisition from empty liquor bottles and from check breakdown for wines. Leave empty bottles with requisition for opening bartender.

BEER SERVICE

Beer is a brewed beverage prepared from barley or rice and flavored with hops. The hops give it a bitter flavor. Most American beer is of the lager variety. Lager beer is light, crisp, and effervescent, and should be served at approximately 38°F (3.3°C). European beer is sometimes richer, darker, and more robust, and should be served at 55°F to 58°F (12.8°C to 14.4°C) unless the label reads otherwise.

Figure 7.29. Yard of Ale.

Many varieties of brewed beverages can complement foods. Offering a good selection of beer will enhance the beverage menu. Beer is especially compatible with lunch, but is also quite acceptable as a cocktail, or with meals in lieu of wine. Some interesting beer variations are:

Red Beer: tomato juice and beer
Black Velvet: Guinness Stout and champagne
Stout and Mild: half stout and half beer

When pouring bottled beer, pour slowly down the inside of the glass which, if possible, should be held at a slight angle. Care should be taken not to produce a large "head" of foam in the glass. Glassware must be spotlessly clean, with no greasy film, or the beer will go flat. Some imported beers might have a sediment in the bottom and should not be emptied completely. Beer stock should be rotated to insure freshness and should always be kept out of direct sunlight.

Figure 7.28. Beer Glasses. Pilsner, Footed Boot.

SAKE SERVICE

Sake is a brewed rice-wine with an alcohol content of 17 percent. It is a light and hearty beverage, and with the increasing popularity of Japanese-style restaurants, it seems quite natural to merchandise Sake. This delightful drink will contribute to the ambience of the dining experience while enhancing the flavor of the meal.

Each brand will have a distinctive flavor. There are at least twelve types, ranging from cooking Sake (Mirin) to refined Sake (Seishu). Sake does not improve with age, and there is a lively competition in Japan to be among the first to taste the new Sake of a fresh harvest.

To experience the true essence of the drink, connoisseurs consider it best to serve Sake warm. Mulled at about 100°F (37.5°C), or slightly above the temperature of the body, the vapors enhance the subtlety of the flavor. It can also be served chilled, on the rocks, or in cocktails.

Sake cups were once made of lacquered wood and were so large that they covered the face of the drinkers. This practice ended when a famous Samurai, while "in his cups," had his head chopped off by an unseen enemy. Today Sake is served in a delicate porcelain cup, called *sakazuki*, and poured from a small narrow-mouthed bottle, called a *tokkuri*. The cup is customarily filled to the rim as a sign of largesse. The recipient always holds the cup out to receive the Sake, and never places the cup on the table to be filled. When the guest has had enough, the cup is left full.

TEA SERVICE

Tea generally refers to an infusion made from the leaves of the tea shrub, cultivated in China, Japan, and the East Indies. The leaves, leaf buds, and internodes of the tea plant are cut and cured and classified according to the method of manufacture, some examples being green teas, black tea, or Oolong. The grading of tea is according to leaf size, such as Congou, Orange Pekoe, Pekoe, and Souchong teas. The aromatic beverage is prepared by infusing the fresh tea leaves with freshly boiled water; for convenience, a tea bag or tea ball may be used. Tea can also be brewed from a variety of herbs, barks, and grasses, singly or in combination. All three kinds of tea — black, green, and herbal — can be further flavored and scented with dried flowers such as rose, chrysanthemum, and jasmine. Professional restaurant service is only beginning to explore the rich variety of quality teas available.

Ideally, tea is served in two preheated ceramic teapots with approximately a 12 oz capacity. Preheating takes the chill off of the pot and insures a better brew. One pot is used for the infusion, which should be allowed to steep for three or four minutes, and the other pot for water. The guest first pours the desired amount of the infusion into the cup, then adds hot water to the desired strength. Herbal teas should also be served in this fashion. They do not tend to become as bitter with oversteeping as regular tea. Both pots are presented on underliners, with a lemon garnish. Wrap the lemon in cheesecloth to avoid seeds falling into the cup and the squirting of juice in unwanted places. A heated cup is served on a saucer. The guest always pours. Since the richness of cream will cover the delicate flavor of tea, milk is the recommended accompaniment in lieu of lemon. If only one pot is served, the tea bag should be served on the side so that the guest can control the desired strength.

The following are some points to remember in the proper storage of all teas:

Keep tea in a dry, clean, and covered container.

Keep tea containers away from moisture.

Keep tea containers away from any strong-smelling foods, as tea quickly absorbs odors.

Iced tea should be made before service. A regular stronger brew can be prepared daily and allowed to cool to room temperature. This brew, if chilled, will become cloudy, so it is advised to serve from room temperature, on ice cubes, in a tall tumbler with lemon and iced teaspoon. An infusion can also be prepared by placing the tea bags in cold water and steeping approximately one or two hours. This, too, should not be refrigerated, as it will cloud. Should iced tea become cloudy in the pitcher, add a bit of hot or boiling water to clear it.

COFFEE SERVICE

Coffee is a tropical evergreen shrub that produces a cherry-type bean, which becomes ripe three or four times a year. Its name derives from the Arabic *Gahwah* or *Kaffa*, a province in Southwest Ethiopia reputed to be where coffee was first used as a beverage.

Arab legend has it that Kaldi, an Abyssinian goat herder, observed his goats eating the berries and noticed the uncommon frivolity that ensued afterwards. Then Kaldi, too, tasted the berries and experienced an exhilarating feeling himself. Eventually, as word spread,

Figure 7.30. Tea Cozy from The Bull and Bear at The Waldorf-Astoria, New York City.

monks brewed the bean in hot water and coffee was discovered, in approximately 850 AD.

A number of points should be observed when storing and holding coffee:

Store coffee in a well-ventilated storeroom.

Use airtight or vacuum packing for ground coffee to insure that coffee oils do not evaporate, causing loss of flavor and strength. Coffee may be kept in the freezer if it is not going to be used quickly.

Rotate stock and check date of grinding on bags.

Do not store coffee close to strong-smelling foods.

When possible, grind the coffee from beans only as needed. Coffee is like a peppercorn: it loses much of its aroma soon after grinding, and is always superior when used freshly ground.

In order to bring out the flavor and quality of the coffee bean, coffee must be properly roasted. Too light a roast results in a thin and characterless product; the darker the roast, the more robust and less bitter the flavor. American roast is the lightest. Espresso is the darkest, with many variations in between, such as Vienna, French, and New Orleans.

Early in the 1900s, Dr. Ludwiz Roelius Agerman developed a process of steaming unroasted coffee beans with the chemical solvent benzine. This process extracted the caffeine from the beans which, when roasted, he called *sans caffine*, from the French for "without caffeine."

Decaffeinated coffee can be purchased in the form of beans for grinding, ground, or powdered instant. Ideally, fresh-brewed should be served. If hot beverages are controlled in the pantry, this system is easily adaptable. If the instant packets are used, they should be emptied into a preheated individual coffee pot and the water added in the kitchen. The pot is served on an underliner with a heated cup. Some operators serve the packet with the water in the dining room to insure the guest of a decaffeinated product. This practice is not recommended, however, since most guests would prefer to be served in better style.

Making Coffee

Careful following of certain steps will assure the best in coffee preparation:

Use freshly-roasted-and-ground high quality coffee beans.

Purchase the proper grind for the coffee machine.

Make sure all the equipment and pots are clean.

Use the recommended proportion of coffee to water.

Figure 7.31. Espresso and Filter Pots.

Control the temperature. Coffee is best brewed at 205°F (96°C) and held at 185°F (90.5°C). Once brewed, never boil coffee or it will have a bitter flavor.

Equipment should meet the needs of the dining room.

Preparing coffee by the pot is recommended for most operations. Large urns are best left for banquets and institutional uses. The fresher the brew, the better the product. Coffee should be served in a metal or pre-heated ceramic pot. The cups should be preheated. Cream and sugar generally accompany coffee and should be on the table before the coffee is served.

Espresso coffee is Italian in origin. Machines used for espresso prepare individual portions of coffee in seconds. The coffee must be finely ground. Steam is forced through the grounds infusing the coffee under pressure. The advantage, of course, is that each cup is freshly prepared. Taken black, the coffee is known as espresso, and is served in a demitasse; with the addition of steamed milk, it becomes cappuccino or French cafe au lait. The popularity of these items in the United States is increasing due to the superiority of the product and method of preparation.

Making Espresso

Follow these steps for making espresso:

1. Check temperature and pressure gauge of the machine.
2. Add coffee to the filter.
3. Tamper or press down the grounds into the filter.
4. Insert filter into machine.
5. Press button to start steam infusion.
6. Serve in demitasse.

Making Cappuccino

Proceed as follows to make cappuccino:

1-5. Follow steps one through five for espresso and continue as follows.
6. Steam milk.
7. Add steamed milk to coffee.
8. Garnish with cinnamon.
9. Serve in standard coffee cup.

Figure 7.32. Making Espresso.

Step a. Espresso machine.

Step b. Check temperature and pressure gauges.

Step c. Add coffee to the filter.

Step d. Tamp down grounds into the filter.

Step e. Insert filter into the machine.

Step f. Press button to start steam infusion.

Figure 7.33. Making Cappucino.

Step a. Steam milk.

Step b. Add steamed milk to coffee (made by same method as espresso).

Step c. Garnish with cinnamon.

BOTTLED MINERAL WATER

Bottled mineral water is hard water. Some experts regard hard water as being healthier to drink than the soft variety. This is due in part to the presence of trace elements in hard water, and also to the fact that it is not treated or purified with chlorine or softened with sodium. Some pollutants in tap water are causing concern to health officials. Certain viruses, heavy metals, and chlorine derivatives are suspect. Hard water is better for teeth, bones, and blood vessels. Do not confuse distilled, processed, or formulated water with bottled mineral water. Distilled water is generally tap water that has been purified through distillation and stripped of its trace minerals.

The consumption of bottled water in the United States is gaining in popularity. Promoting the sales of bottled mineral water will:

Increase the check average

Enhance the dining experience

Contribute to a sense of style about the operation

Every operation will have its own manner of serving water. There are certain aspects of water service, however, that should remain constant:

Refrigerate the water to 38°F (3.3°C).

Never serve ice or lime wedge unless requested.

Ideally, open the bottle at the table.

To create interest in the beverage list, offer various sizes and types of water.

Large bottles of mineral water can remain on the table.

Bottled mineral water can be served at various times throughout the meal. To promote sales, suggest it:

When a cocktail is not ordered

As a mixer with spirit or wine

During or after dinner to refresh the palate

8
MERCHANDISING IN THE DINING ROOM

To merchandise is to promote the sale of a product. Restaurant patrons are a captive audience who actually want to be sold products and entertained with interesting and ingenious displays. Many dramatic exhibitions can be used by restaurateurs to captivate attention at table, such as gueridon service, sous cloche and en papillote presentations, voiture service, flambeing, and cigar or other specialty services. The many distinctive pieces of equipment that are available for use in the dining room help to establish ambience, which encourages the guest to order items that will create a unique dining experience. A list of such equipment would include: gueridons, fondu sets, jambon holders, bar carts, fish poachers, carving utensils, souffle dishes, specialty tableware and barware, ramekins, sabayon sets, and café brulot sets. Appeal can also be created with food displays in the dining room, such as a cold poached salmon, or roast prime rib of beef carved and plated in the dining area or at buffets and soup stations.

All categories of the menu can be highlighted with showmanship, special equipment, or displays, but management must evaluate the clientele and establish which specialty items would complement their particular menu. The service staff must be able to handle these highlighted items comfortably. Special training in tableside cookery and the use of specialized equipment may be necessary to develop proficiency and style.

THE GUERIDON

One of the most effective methods of merchandising in the dining room is gueridon service. The original definition of "gueridon" was a small round table with folding sides. Today, a gueridon is generally a rectangular table mounted on wheels. As such, the gueridon is ideal for transporting food directly from the kitchen to the table, thereby eliminating a stop at the side or tray stands. Gueridons are commonly used for setting up food displays and for the tableside preparation of the salad, fruit and cheese, and dessert courses. With the addition of a heating device, known as a rechaud, the gueridon is especially suited for tableside cookery. Some suitable items for gueridon service are soups from tureens, and poached salmon in aspic; pasta, freshly cooked in the kitchen and sauced in the dining room; meats, fish, game, and poultry that lend themselves to rapid cooking; crepes, sweets, and fruits in combination with ice creams and other ingredients. Be adventuresome and create house speciality items.

Gueridon service can be used exclusively in an a la carte operation, or it can be incorporated into any type of table service with a standard prix fixe or table d'hote menu. The total use of the gueridon is very genteel and lends itself to gracious dining. It eliminates trays being carried through the dining room and also does away

99

with tray stands. However the gueridon is used, its proper selection will depend on these factors:

Ambience of the dining room: The design of the cart and the dining room must complement each other.

The functions the cart will be required to perform: For example, a gueridon to be used for tableside cookery might require a permanent rechaud.

The physical limitations of the dining room: Where aisle space is at a premium, a narrower gueridon or perhaps one which is stationary might be necessary.

Gueridons can be purchased with a drop leaf at either end. With the drop leaf in a down position, the gueridon can be more easily moved through the dining room and the amount of required storage space is reduced. Gueridons with one or two shelves under the work surface ensure adequate space for mise en place, clean flatware, napery, serviceware, and soiled tableware. Gueridons are often designed with a brake mechanism so that the gueridon can be held stationary. This is especially useful when the gueridon will be heavily loaded. Trolleys, similar to gueridons, are tiered carts which can be used to display and serve hors d'oeuvres, salads, desserts, or other cold foods.

Figure 8.2. Gueridon with Sterno Rechaud.

Figure 8.3. Gueridon with Alcohol Rechaud.

Figure 8.1. Gueridon.

Figure 8.4. Gueridon Dressed for Salad Service.

Figure 8.5. Gueridon Dressed for Fruit and Cheese Service.

Figure 8.6. Trolley.

TABLESIDE COOKERY

Tableside cookery is not only an excellent method of merchandising; it also provides dining room staff with an opportunity to exhibit showmanship and display their acquired professional skills. Carried out in the proper setting and with the proper equipment, tableside cookery reaches the level of a performing art. All the while, though, the performer must keep in mind that the drama must come second to the preparation of the food. The most skilled performance will be a failure if the resulting food is not prepared to perfection. On the other hand, exquisite food, flawlessly prepared in an entertaining and artful manner, is the sign of a true professional.

To make certain that the extra effort exerted for tableside cookery is properly staged, the right equipment must be purchased. Speciality sets are available for specific dishes such as sabayon and cafe brulot. While the use of specialty equipment can add an extra element of style to tableside preparation, simple, unaffected equipment will often be more than adequate. Because tableside cookery draws the attention of the whole dining room to the production area, make sure that the equipment is clean and operates adequately for the tasks to be performed.

Rechauds

The heat needed for tableside cookery is provided by a cooking lamp known as a rechaud. Some gueridons are constructed with a well into which the rechaud can be set. In the absence of such a well, the rechaud can simply be placed on the top shelf of the gueridon.

Fuel for the rechauds comes in three common forms: liquid (alcohol), solid (sterno), and gas (butane or propane). Alcohol creates a high intensity flame which is required for dishes like omelettes or crêpes. Wood alcohol is purer and burns longer than denatured alcohol, although it emits an odor when burning.

Sterno is alcohol in a jellied form. Being a solid, it cannot spill and is considered the safest of fuels. However, sterno does not burn as hot as liquid alcohol and is more difficult to regulate. It is ideal for use with chafing dishes to keep cooked foods hot.

Butane and propane have been recently developed for dining room burners. They provide heat that is longer lasting and less dangerous than alcohol. They are very easy to regulate, but emit a sound which can be distracting. The capsules hold enough fuel for approximately 1-1/4 hours of tableside cooking, but are not equipped with a gauge to indicate when fuel is running out.

Each day, as part of the regular mise en place, check whatever heat source is used. The heating elements should be examined for cleanliness, for adequate fuel supply, and, when applicable, to assure a sufficient wick for the upcoming meal period or that the gas jet is not clogged.

Pans

There are two types of general purpose pans used for tableside cookery — the crepe or suzette pan, and the flambe pan. Other specialty equipment is available for more defined purposes such as cherries jubilee or cafe diable sets. Whether all purpose or specific, dining room cookware should be both functional and attractive.

The crepe pan is usually made of copper or copper with a stainless steel lining. It is approximately ten to twelve inches wide and one inch deep, making it perfect for flaming, folding, and stacking crepes before plating. This crepe pan should not be confused with the kitchen crepe pan, which is used to cook the crepe batter.

Deeper than the crepe pan is the flambe pan, which can be up to two and one-half inches deep. It comes in various shapes — round, oval, and rectangular. The flambe pan is used when more room is needed to work comfortably, without fear of spilling or splattering.

Serviceware

Serving spoons and forks are always used to work with food items on the gueridon. They become an extension of the waiter's hand and must be as flexible as required by the job to be performed. There are two basic ways of using serving forks and spoons:

1. The fork is maneuvered in one hand and the spoon in the other. This method is used to transfer food from the platter to the pan or bowl, and then to the plate for serving. It is also used to add ingredients as required by the recipe, or to "napper" (coat) an item with sauce once the food has been plated.

2. Both the fork and spoon are manipulated in the same hand, like a pair of tongs. This method is used in Russian service when serving food from a tray or platter.

Knives

Most cutting and slicing on the gueridon can be accomplished with a utility knife. The blade is generally narrow, sturdy, and seven to eight inches long. For slicing large items, a ten to twelve inch blade is preferred. A boning knife may be required for boning poultry. A paring knife is often used for small jobs such as carving and peeling fruit.

Figure 8.7. Oval and Round Suzette Pans.

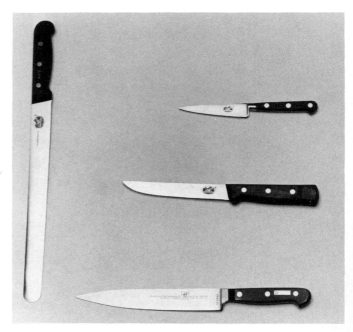

Figure 8.8. Knives Used on the Gueridon: Slicer, Paring Knife, Boning Knife, and Utility Knife.

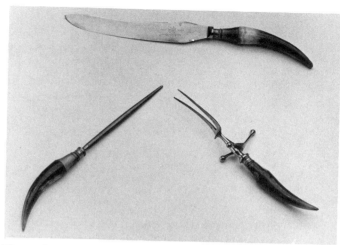

Figure 8.9. Dining Room Carving Utensils: Slicer, Steel, and Fork.

Figure 8.10. Flambe Swords Equipped with Cups for Alcohol.

Steel

The steel is used to restore the edge of a knife blade which has been blunted during cutting or slicing. This is a maintenance tool and is not meant to replace a sharpening stone, which actually hones the blade. The steel is used between sharpenings on the stone and immediately after each sharpening.

Steeling should be performed in the kitchen as part of the mise en place, since the noise of this activity may be undesirable in a fine dining room. An exception would be if there is a permanent carving station in the dining room, or if the steeling of the blade is incorporated into a dining room display for the entertainment of the guests. Directions for using the steel are as follows:

When stroking the knife across the steel, use a gentle easy movement. The right amount of pressure will produce a melodic sound; too much pressure creates a grinding noise.

The blade and the steel should meet at a 20 degree angle.

Do not oversteel the knife. Five or six strokes on each side of the blade is sufficient. If the blade is still not as sharp as it should be, use a sharpening stone.

Always try to use a steel which has a guard on the handle, and be sure to position your fingers, especially your thumb, behind the guard.

Carving Boards and Surfaces

There are essentially four types of carving boards and surfaces: wood, marble, hard rubber, and plastic. Some factors to consider when selecting a surface are cleanability, resilience, and the particular job to be done. For tableside service, the design and appearance are also important.

Wood is the most popular of all carving surfaces. It is resilient, can be used for most any type of tableside preparation, and it makes an appealing presentation. Some care must be taken to sanitize the wooden surface properly.

While marble is easy to clean, it is rather hard and has little resilience. Because the surface is so cool and does not absorb odors as quickly as other types of surfaces, marble is particularly suitable for the presentation of such items as cheese or poached or smoked salmon. Marble is also quite attractive. However, it is not suitable as an all-purpose surface.

Hard rubber is easy to clean and sanitize and is very resilient. For tableside service, however, the color is too dull, and it is not as attractive as wood or marble.

Plastic meets all requirements for cleanliness, but it has little resilience and does develop ruts and chips. Also, cutting marks left from carving have a tendency to discolor and spoil the appearance of the surface.

TABLESIDE RECIPES

When developing a menu, be careful not to overwork the concept of tableside cookery. It is best to highlight, not congest, the menu with this high-styled service or it will soon lose its impact. In addition, too many tableside items may create service problems and lead to the neglect of regular items.

Most tableside preparations are promotionally and gastronomically sound. However, some recipes are not as suitable as others to tableside cookery. An item such as Beef Stroganoff might create a problem if prepared tableside. The recipe calls for the sauteing of onions, which would impart a strong aroma to all guests in the dining room, some of whom might be about to begin a delicate souffle. Flambe work also creates food odors and sometimes alcohol or gas fumes, which are not desirable in a fine dining room. For this reason, flaming should be kept to a minimum on the menu.

Recipes for tableside cookery should be designed for the swift preparation of food. The service person cannot spend valuable time away from the other tables, and the aroma of prolonged cooking in the dining room may disturb the other guests. Avoid half-cooking food in the kitchen and finishing it in the dining room. If the recipe does not lend itself to total dining room preparation, eliminate it from consideration, as the end result will be inferior due to precooking.

Classical recipes are often used as the basis for developing a menu for tableside cookery. Such menu items as Steak au Poivre, Caesar Salad, and Crepes Suzette have become standard fare. Keep in mind, however, that innovation should always be encouraged. Adapt classical recipes and create totally new dishes to respond to the demands of your clientele.

When adapting creative interpretations of classical recipes, be sure to establish precise, standard house recipes for these items. All service personnel must know and adhere to these standard recipes to ensure a consistent product. Patrons need to be guaranteed that the Cherries Jubilee they are ordering now will taste like the Cherries Jubilee they ordered last week.

When establishing house recipes, be sure to include all necessary equipment, ingredients, amounts, and methods of preparation. List the ingredients in the order used. If the item is to be sold "for two" only, give the amount for two portions; otherwise, all amounts should be calculated for a single portion. Finally, list the method of preparation step-by-step. Comprehensive recipes will not only ensure consistency, but will also serve as an aid when training new personnel.

FLAMING DISHES (FLAMBE)

Flaming dishes are particularly appealing to the American public. Management promotes flamed items because they command premium prices — flaming a dish automatically raises the menu price. Service personnel enjoy flaming dishes as a creative outlet. The process of flaming is not always gastronomically sound, however, and can sometimes be dangerous.

Aside from emitting odors throughout the dining room, flaming can often adversely change the flavor of food. This is particularly true when too much liquor is added to create a larger flame. Overflaming is hazardous, and it not only alters the taste of the food but also can prove quite costly, as liquor is an expensive item. Adhering to the following procedures will ensure theatrical effects without excessively high costs and undo harm to the food:

- Add spirits with the flambe or suzette pan off the fire and turned away from the guest. An alternate approach would be to pour the spirit into a small wide-mouthed container, and then add it to the pan. This eliminates any chance that the bottle of spirit will explode.
- Ignite the flame by tilting the pan so that the liquor's vapor touches the rechaud flame. Never use a match or lighter. Another approach is to coat a spoon with liquor, ignite the spoon with the rechaud flame, and then ignite the rest of the liquor in the pan with the lit spoon.
- Do not overpour for sensational effect. Flaming excessive spirits is dangerous, harmful to food, and expensive.
- Flames can easily be extinguished by smothering them with a lid or by the addition of nonalcoholic liquid such as cream or sauce.
- Fortified wines and low proof spirits must be undiluted and preferably somewhat heated before flaming or else they will not ignite.
- For a special effect with sweet desserts, sprinkle sugar into the flame to change the flame's color.
- As flaming has little effect on the actual temperature of the food, be sure all food is adequately cooked and very hot prior to flaming.

The process of flaming, besides being showy, also serves the purpose of cooking away the alcohol of the spirit added to the recipe. If the dish will not be flamed, cut back on the amount of spirit added.

PREPARING GUERIDON FOR SERVICE

The gueridon must be properly prepared for tableside cookery prior to service. Before dressing the gueridon examine it for stability. Check the wheels to make certain that the gueridon will roll evenly. Examine the brake mechanism to be sure that gueridon will remain stationary when needed. Once the gueridon has passed this simple inspection, clean it from top to bottom.

The top shelf should be covered with a small table-cloth folded to the exact size of the unit. Do not allow the cloth to extend over the edges, as it may catch on something while the gueridon is in motion, causing an accident. If there is a hole cut out for the rechaud, make sure the tablecloth fits under the metal ring. This will secure the cloth and prevent it from slipping directly into the flame. If a portable rechaud is used, the cloth will prevent the rechaud from slipping.

The lower shelves should be attractively and neatly dressed with linen napkins or tablecloths. These shelves should be adequately stocked with serving forks and spoons, carving knives, underliners, folded napkins, and whatever mise en place will be needed for service.

The food needed to prepare a tableside order is generally added to the top shelf of the gueridon during service, just prior to wheeling the gueridon from the kitchen into the dining room. When restaurants offer only one tableside item per day on the menu, generally featured as a special, nonperishable food items such as Worcestershire sauce, dried and prepared mustard, spirits, spices, and seasonings may be stored on the gueridon before service begins. These items should be kept on the middle shelf, out of the way when the gueridon is being used for other purposes, and then moved to the top shelf just before the tableside preparation.

When possible, the correct portion size of ingre-dients should be set on the gueridon. For example, if a recipe calls for two slices of meat per order, set two slices for each order at the table; do not stock more or less than will be needed. However, if the recipe calls for three tablespoons of grated cheese, stock a whole cup of grated cheese and measure the three tablespoons at service. Arrange all ingredients neatly and in the order which they will be added to the recipe. This will ensure the quality and consistency of the finished product.

The gueridon should be completely set before it is wheeled to the table, where it is positioned for easy viewing by the guests. Be sure to leave enough room to work comfortably, but avoid blocking traffic aisles. Light and extinguish the rechaud at tableside. Flames may go out if the cart is moved after the rechaud has been lit. Moving an ignited rechaud also poses safety hazards.

When working at the gueridon, stand erect with a smile, and maintain eye contact with the guests. No verbal explanation of the process being performed is

necessary unless the guests request the information. Work quietly, neatly, and smoothly. Once an item has been used in the tableside preparation, remove it from the top shelf and set it on one of the lower shelves. Keep all movements smooth and graceful — not too fast and not too slow. Once the food has been cooked, plate it quickly so that the guests receive the food at its peak. Position and garnish the food artistically. When serving hot food use warmed plates; when serving cold foods use chilled plates.

Fettucine Carbonara. This is fettucine cooked in the style of the coal makers of Italy. To serve fettucine carbonara for two, you will need a gueridon, a rechaud, and a suzette pan. For ingredients the following amounts will yield one appetizer order. Double them for a main course. Have ready 1½ oz (43 g) butter, 6 oz (170 g) cooked fettucine, ground black pepper (to be added to taste), 2 tbsp (30 ml) chopped cooked bacon, 1 egg yolk, 4 oz (114 g) heavy cream, and 3 tbsp (45 ml) parmesan cheese. More cheese may be offered once the fettucine has been plated.

Caesar Salad (For Two). While recipes for the sauce may vary, the greens should always be Romaine lettuce. For equipment, you will need a gueridon, and a wooden salad bowl. For ingredients for two servings, assemble 3 anchovies, 1 clove garlic, ½ tsp (2.5 ml) olive oil, 1 tsp (5 ml) dry or Dijon mustard, ½ lemon, 1 coddled egg, 1/3 head Romaine lettuce, ground black pepper (to be added to taste), 3 tbsp (45 ml) parmesan cheese, and 3 tbsp (45 ml) croutons.

Figure 8.11. Fettucini Carbonara.

Step a. Mise en place: butter, fettucini, black pepper, bacon, egg, cream, parmesan cheese, and a suzette pan.

Step b. Add butter to pan.

Step c. When butter has melted, add the fettucini.

Step d. Add freshly ground black pepper.

Step e. Add chopped, cooked bacon.

Step f. Mix.

Step g. Break an egg and separate the yolk.

Step h. Add the yolk to the cream.

Step i. Stir yolk into cream, creating a liaison.

Step j. Add the liaison.

Step k. Sprinkle with parmesan cheese.

Step l. Toss the fettucini to evenly distribute the sauce.

Step m. Plate and serve.

Figure 8.12. Caesar Salad.

Step a. Mise en place: garlic, anchovies, olive oil, mustard, lemon, coddled egg, pepper, parmesan cheese, croutons, Romaine lettuce, and a salad bowl.

Step b. Place a clove of garlic into a salad bowl.

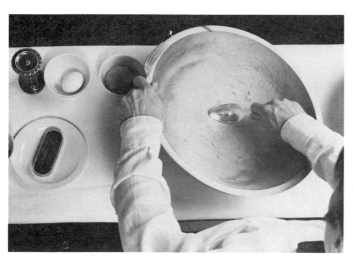

Step c. Mash the garlic into a paste with a serving spoon.

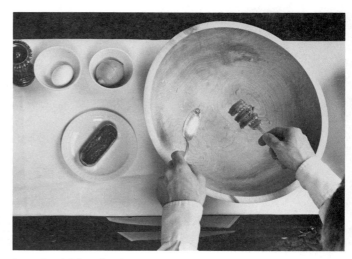

Step d. Add anchovies.

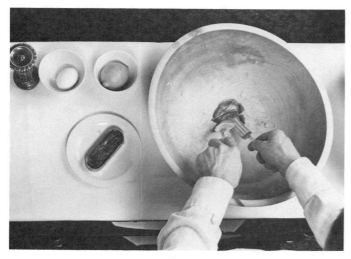

Step e. Mash anchovies into a paste.

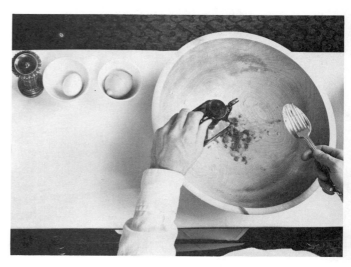

Step f. Add olive oil.

Step g. Incorporate the olive oil into the paste.

Step h. Add mustard and mix.

Step i. Add lemon juice.

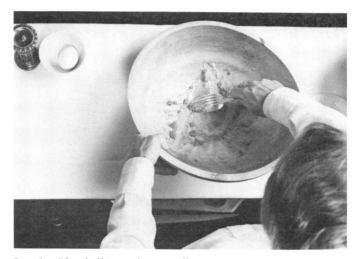

Step j. Blend all ingredients well.

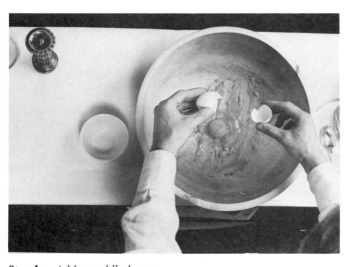

Step k. Add a coddled egg.

Step l. Blend all ingredients well.

Step m. Add Romaine lettuce to the bowl.

Step n. Cut the leaves with the fork and spoon.

Step o. Toss the lettuce with the dressing. Work toward you to avoid splattering onto the guests.

Step p. Add freshly ground pepper.

Step q. Add parmesan cheese.

Step r. Toss together once again.

Step s. Add croutons.

Step t. Toss.

Step u. Plate and serve.

Canard Montmorency. If Grand Marnier is substituted for Kirsch, and Bigarade Sauce for Cherry Sauce, the dish becomes Canard Bigarade. To prepare this dish, you will need a gueridon, a rechaud, a carving board, a carving knife, and a suzette pan. Ingredients for two servings will comprise 1 cooked duckling, 3 oz (85 g) Kirsch, and 6 oz (170 g) bing cherry sauce (prepared earlier).

Saltimbocca Romana. "Saltimbocca," translated literally, means to "jump in the mouth." This dish is said to be so tasty that it almost seems to jump from the pan into the mouth. For equipment, you will need a gueridon, a rechaud, and a suzette pan. For ingredients, assemble 2 slices veal scallopini, 2 slices very thin prosciutto, ground black pepper (to be added to taste), 1½ oz (43 g) clarrified butter, a pinch sage, 1½ oz (43 g) Marsala wine, and 4 oz (114 g) fond de veau lie.

Figure 8.13. Canard Montmorency.

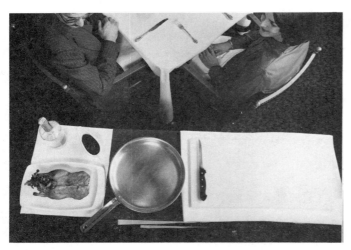

Step a. Mise en place: cooked duckling, kirsch, bing cherry sauce, carving knife, and a suzette pan.

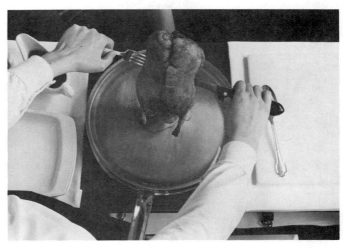

Step b. Drain fat from duck into pan.

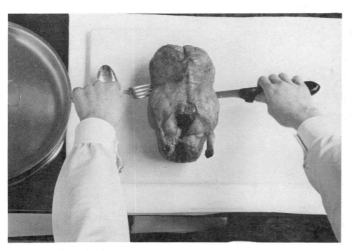

Step c. Place duck onto carving board.

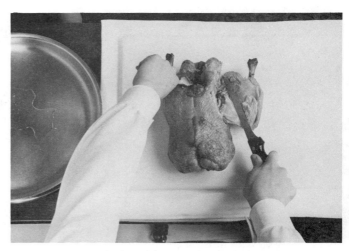

Step d. Remove thigh and leg together and place into pan.

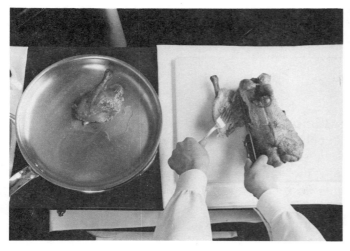

Step e. Remove second thigh and leg and add to pan.

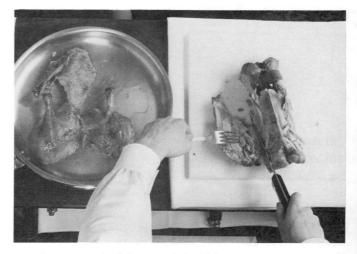

Step f. Remove both breasts and add them to pan. Allow duck to heat in pan.

Step g. Remove pan from fire. Tilt it away from guests and add kirsch.

Step h. Return pan to fire. Tilt front of pan toward flame, igniting alcohol vapors.

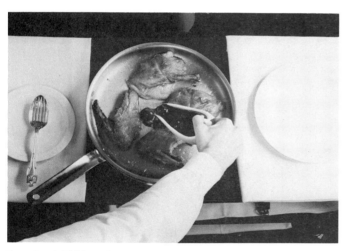

Step i. Add bing cherry sauce.

Step j. Stir.

Step k. Spoon sauce onto plate.

Step l. Place duck over sauce. Add accompaniments and serve.

Figure 8.14. Saltimbocca Romana.

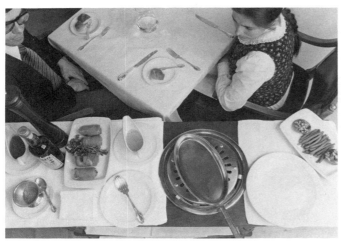

Step a. Mise en place: clarified butter, prosciutto rolled in veal, pepper, sage, Marsala wine, fond de veau, and a suzette pan.

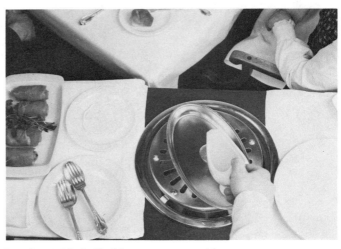

Step b. Add clarified butter to pan and heat.

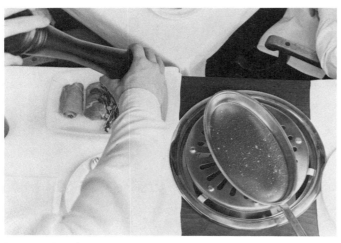

Step c. Grind pepper over veal.

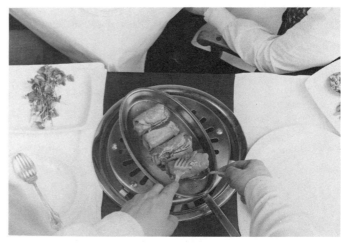

Step d. Add veal to pan. Saute on all sides. Turn as needed.

Step e. Sprinkle with sage.

Step f. Add more pepper.

Step g. Remove pan from fire. Tilt it away from guests and add Marsala.

Step h. Return pan to fire. Add fond de veau. Cook until done, basting as needed.

Step i. Plate veal. Add sauce and accompaniments. Serve.

Steak au Poivre. The black pepper used for Steak au Poivre should always be of the coarse-ground variety known as mignonette. For equipment, have ready a gueridon, a rechaud, and a suzette pan. For ingredients, assemble two 3 to 4 oz (57 to 114 g) tournedos of fillet of beef, or 6 to 9 oz (170 to 228 g) strip sirloin steak, 2 tbsp (30 ml) coarse ground black pepper, 1½ oz (43 g) butter, 1½ oz (43 g) Cognac, 1 tsp (5 ml) Dijon mustard, 3 oz (85 g) fond de veau lie, a few dashes worcestershire sauce, and 2 oz (57 g) heavy cream.

Cherries Jubilee. This dessert is made with Kirsch, a spirit distilled from fermented, ripe wild cherries. For

Figure 8.15. Steak au Poivre.

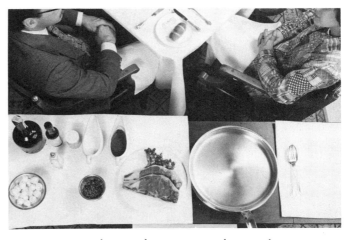

Step a. Mise en place: steak, coarse-ground pepper, butter, cognac, Dijon mustard, fond de veau, worcestershire sauce, cream, and a suzette pan.

Step b. Spoon pepper over steaks.

Step c. Press pepper into steaks.

Step d. Add butter to pan.

Step e. Add steaks to pan — pepper side down.

Step f. Spoon more pepper over steaks.

Step g. Press pepper into steaks.

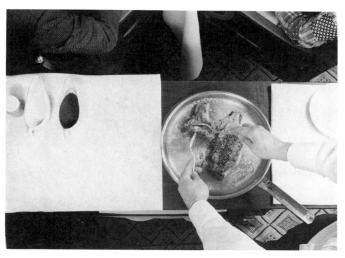

Step h. Turn steaks to cook other side.

Step i. Remove pan from fire. Tilt pan away from guests and add cognac or brandy. Return pan to fire.

Step j. When steaks have been cooked to order, remove them from pan. Cover to keep hot.

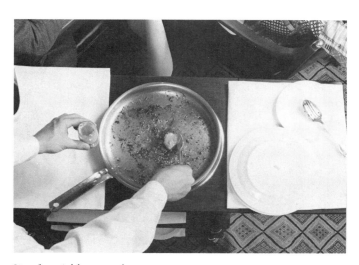

Step k. Add mustard to pan.

Step l. Add fond de veau.

Step m. Add worcestershire sauce. Mix and cook sauce.

Step n. Add cream and mix.

Step o. Return steaks to pan briefly to cook with sauce.

Step p. Plate steaks.

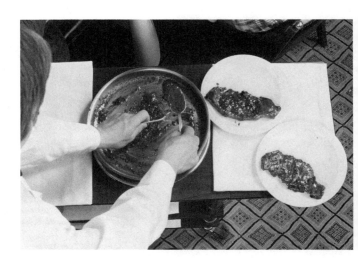

Step q. Coat with sauce and serve.

Figure 8.16. Cherries Jubilee.

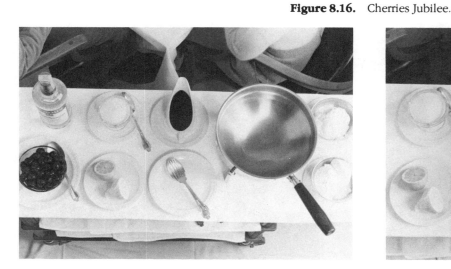

Step a. Mise en place: cherry juice, lemon, sugar, bing cherries, kirsch, vanilla ice cream, cherries jubilee set.

Step b. Pour cherry juice.

Step c. Add lemon juice. (Lemon has been wrapped in cheese-cloth to prevent pits from falling into juice.)

Step d. Add sugar.

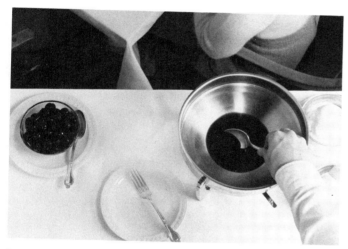

Step e. Stir to dissolve sugar.

Step f. Add cherries.

Step g. Remove pan from fire. Tilt away from guests and add kirsch.

Step h. Dip spoon into pan and remove a small amount of liquid. Ignite the liquid from the flame of the heating unit.

Step i. Raise the flaming spoon.

Step j. Ignite the liquid in the pan.

Step k. Spoon cherries and sauce over ice cream. Serve.

Figure 8.17. Crepes Suzette.

equipment, you will need a gueridon, a rechaud, and a cherries jubilee set or a suzette pan. For ingredients for two servings, assemble 6 oz (170 g) cherry juice, ½ lemon, 1 tbsp (15 ml) sugar, about 24 bing cherries, 3 oz (85 g) Kirsch, and 2 dishes vanilla ice cream.

Crepes Suzette. This is possibly the most popular way in the world of serving dessert crepes. For equipment, you will need a gueridon, a rechaud, a knife, a zester, and a suzette pan. For two servings, assemble 2 tbsp (30 ml) sugar, 2 oz (57 g) sweet butter, 1 orange, 1 lemon, 4 crepes, and 3 oz (85 g) Grand Marnier.

Step a. Mise en place: sugar, butter, orange, lemon, crepes, Grand Marnier, and suzette pan.

Step b. Add sugar to pan and caramelize.

Step c. Add butter.

Step d. Melt butter and blend with caramelized sugar.

Step e. Add zest of lemon.

Step f. Add zest of orange.

Step g. Insert fork into lemon.

Step h. Squeeze lemon and extract juice by raising and lowering fork.

Step i. Repeat with orange.

Step j. Stir sauce.

Step k. Add crepe to pan. Release the crepe away from the guests to prevent sauce from splattering in their direction.

Step l. Turn crepe over to coat both sides with sauce. All actions should be toward you, not in the direction of the guests.

Step m. Fold crepe in half.

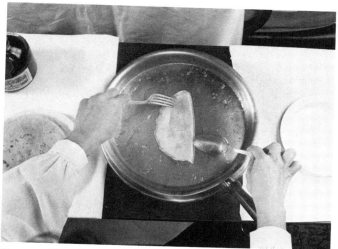

Step n. Turn folded crepe 90 degrees.

Step o. Fold into quarters.

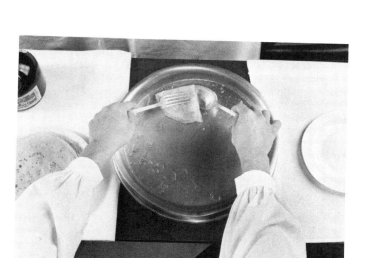

Step p. Position folded crepe toward front of pan.

Step q. Repeat with three more crepes.

Step r. Reposition the crepes in the center of the pan.

Step s. Remove pan from fire. Tilt it away from guests and add Grand Marnier.

Step t.   Return pan to fire. Tilt front of pan toward flame to ignite alcohol vapors.

Step u.   Plate crepes.

Step v.   Spoon over sauce and serve.

Irish Coffee (For Two).   Heavy cream may be substituted for whipped cream. In either case apply the cream in the same way. Have ready a gueridon, a rechaud, two Irish coffee glasses, and two linen napkins.

For two servings, you will need 2 tsp (10 ml) brown sugar, 3 oz (85 g) Irish whiskey, 10 oz (283 g) hot coffee, (double strength may be used), and 4 tbsp (60 ml) whipped cream.

Figure 8.18.   Irish Coffee.

Step a.   Mise en place: brown sugar, whiskey, coffee, whipped cream, glasses, and linen napkins.

Step b.   Add sugar to glasses.

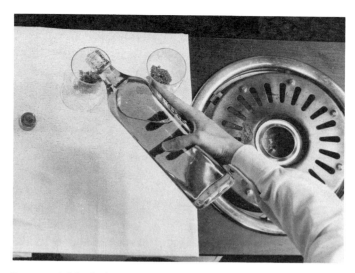

Step c. Add whiskey.

Step d. Grasp base of glass. Hold bowl of glass over flame to dissolve sugar. Caution: glass will become hot.

Step e. Pour hot coffee into glasses.

Step f. Warm a spoon over flame.

Step g. Tip each glass with a dollop of whipped cream. Warm spoon will allow cream to fall easily on top of coffee.

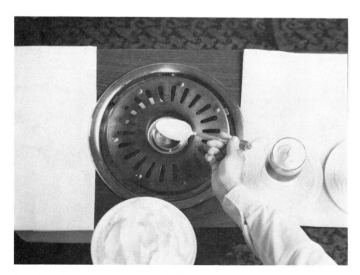

Step h. Warm spoon as needed.

Step i. Finish topping with whipped cream, taking care not to mix it with coffee.

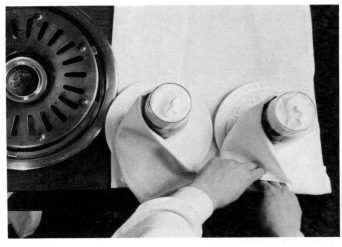

Step j. Wrap each hot glass with a linen napkin and serve.

Figure 8.19. Cafe Diable.

Cafe Diable. When Grand Marnier is used in place of Kahlua, this dessert beverage is known as Cafe Brulot. To make cafe diable for two, have ready a gueridon, a cafe diable set with ladle, a knife, and two cups. Ingredients for two servings will comprise 2 tsp (10 ml) sugar, 1 cinnamon stick, 1 lemon peel, 1 orange peel, 6 to 8 cloves, 1½ oz (43 g) Kahlua, 1½ oz (43 g) brandy, and 10 oz (283 g) hot coffee. Double strength coffee may be used if desired.

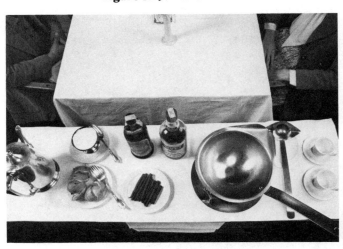

Step a. Mise en place: brandy, Kahlua, sugar, cinnamon, lemon peel, orange peel studded with cloves, coffee, cafe diable set with ladle, and cups.

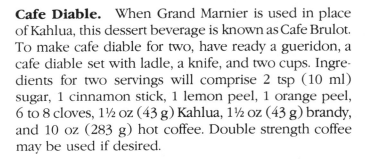

Step b. Pour brandy.

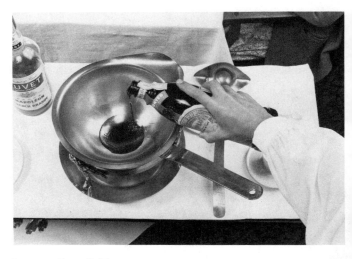

Step c. Pour Kahlua.

Step d. Add sugar.

Step e. Add cinnamon stick.

Step f. Add lemon peel.

Step g. Add orange peel studded with cloves.

Step h. Holding orange peel with fork over cafe diable set, partially fill ladle with hot alcohol mixture and ignite it.

Step i. Ladle flaming liquid down orange peel. Repeat.

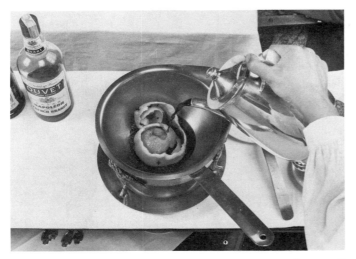

Step j. Return orange peel to cafe diable set and add coffee. Let all ingredients heat for a few minutes.

Step k. Ladle into cups. Serve hot.

OTHER SPECIAL FORMS OF SERVICE

Merchandising occurs in a restaurant whenever special attention is fixed on any saleable item. Special forms of service such as tableside cookery, voiture and cigar service, sous cloche and en papillote presentations and portable tableside bars not only impress the individual party; they also attract the attention of surrounding patrons, who may be prompted to order some specially presented item in place of, or in addition to, their regular order.

En papillote is the practice of cooking and serving food in a sack or bag. This form of preparation and presentation not only arouses interest and attention throughout the dining room, but is also a gastronomical specialty. Subtle essences and aromas are sealed into

Figure 8.21. Voiture at The Palace, New York City.

Figure 8.20. Sous Cloche.

Figure 8.22. Bar Cart at The Palace, New York City.

the swelled sack. When the sack is opened tableside, the fragrant bouquet is suddenly released and the guest inhales a concentration of delicate flavors. En papillote presentations must be handled with grace and style to showcase the release of flavors — the climactic moment of this form of service.

To achieve full effect, a dish cooked en papillote must be served as soon as possible after cooking. Precise timing is needed between kitchen and dining room so that the dish is picked up for service immediately after it is taken from the oven. Once transported into the dining room, the food platter is presented to the guest. The waiter may serve the food directly en papillote and then open the sack at the table, or else set the food on a gueridon where it is carefully opened, plated with the appropriate accompaniments, and served.

Figure 8.23. En Papillote Service.

Step a. Present platter to table.

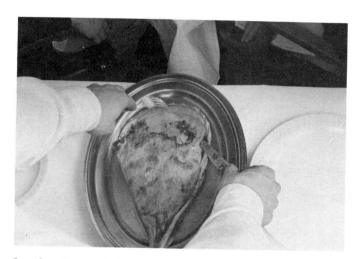

Step b. Return platter to gueridon and cut open paper sack.

Step c. Secure edge of paper in tines of serving fork and roll back paper.

Step d. Completely expose food item (filets of pompano is pictured here).

Step e. Plate filets.

Step f. Add sauce and accompaniments.

Step g. Serve.

Somewhat similar to en papillote service is the sous cloche presentation. Food is fully cooked and arranged on a platter which is then covered with a dome or bell, hence the expression *sous cloche* — "under the bell." The cloche is removed by the waiter directly at table or else on the gueridon, which is positioned tableside. The uncovering provides a visual as well as olfactory sensation for the guest.

Alcoholic beverages in the form of wines, drinks, and beers can also be successfully merchandised in the dining room. A portable bar assembled on a special cart or the versatile gueridon can promote beverage sales through the staging of tableside bartending. The presence of the portable bar cart in the dining room also serves as a constant visual reminder to the guest that drinks are available. Specialty drinks served in specialty glassware often prove to be an effective merchandising technique. Offering a house wine bearing the name and

Figure 8.25. Sushi Bar at Windows on the World, New York City.

Figure 8.24. Cigar Service at The Palace, New York City.

Figure 8.26. Martini Served in a Supreme Set.

logo of the operation is another approach to increasing liquor sales.

Besides food and beverage, tobacco can also be marketed and sold in the dining room. Cigarette and cigar service (see chapter 6) will promote the sale of tobacco while adding an element of style and elegance to the ambience.

SPECIAL EQUIPMENT

Even without a particular manner of presentation, food can be effectively merchandised in the dining room with the use of special equipment for serving. This can be as simple as serving soup in a crock or as involved as employing individual fish poaches for preparing and serving single portions of whole fish. A martini served straight up on crushed ice in a vial and supreme set, and with a chilled glass, can convey an element of

Figure 8.28. Humidor.

Figure 8.27. Marmite for Soup Service.

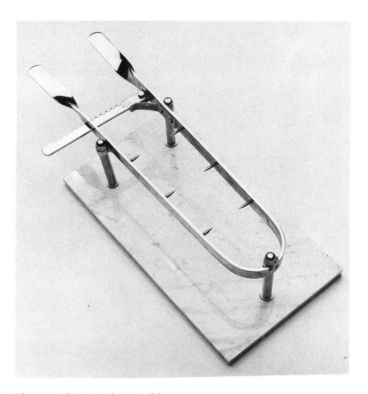

Figure 8.29. Jambon Holder.

Figure 8.30. Sabayon Set.

Figure 8.33. Souffle Dishes.

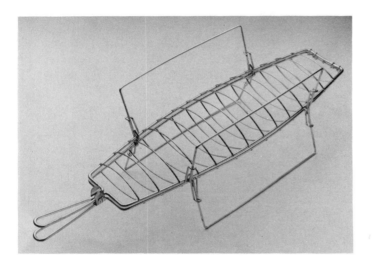

Figure 8.31. Wire Fish Rack.

Figure 8.34. Cafe Diable Set.

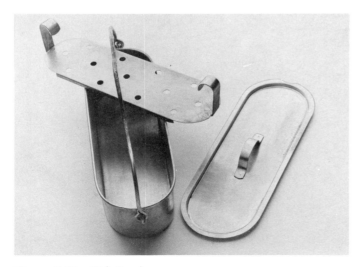

Figure 8.32. Fish Poacher.

Figure 8.35. Soup Cart.

prestige to the guest. A souffle served in an attractive dish takes on an air of elegance. A sabayon prepared tableside in a sabayon set, as opposed to a mixing bowl, adds style and flair to the service. Other special equipment which can be used to promote the sale of particular items are wire fish racks, for finishing a whole cooked fish over burning fennel sticks; jambon holders, used for carving fine hams; marmites, for holding quantities of soup at a soup station, or a smaller version for the individual preparation and service of soup. Special equipment calls attention to itself without the need of any extra labor. However, the visual impact of special equipment will be effective only if the equipment is in good repair and clean.

Figure 8.37. Cafe Tartufo, New York City: House Wine with House Label, Chalkboard Wine List, Posted Specials, and Pasta Display.

DISPLAYS

Displays of food help to sell the product while adding life and excitement to the dining room. They can be designed for self-service, an example being the salad bar, or they can be serviced by an attendant, as with a soup, cheese, or dessert station where a waiter portions and plates the product. Dining room displays can be used to promote any part of the meal:

> Cocktail wagons
> Appetizer trolleys
> Soup carts and stations
> Salad bars

Figure 8.38. Dessert Trolley.

> Cold poached fish displays or lobster and trout tanks
> Meats served en voiture or from a carving station
> Wine carts, racks, or cabinets
> Espresso machines
> Dessert trolleys or stations

The use of these displays not only increases sales, but enhances the appearance of the dining room as well; for this reason they must be artfully and attractively designed and constructed.

Figure 8.36. Buffet at Windows on the World, New York City.

Displays which are purely decorative can also be used in the dining room — salt, ice, and butter sculptures; tallow work; pastillage; pulled sugar; and nougat. In the culinary field, pride is taken in the construction of involved and intricate decorative pieces made entirely from edible materials. However, these showpieces should not be eaten. Although theoretically edible, they are not particularly palatable, and can be reused if properly stored.

One of the most efficient forms of merchandising in both a functional and decorative way is the buffet. The buffet table is a miniature market place attractively displayed to merchandise the food offered. Ice carvings, flower arrangements, tallow or butter sculptures, bread sculptures, and sugar and nougat pieces can be used to draw attention to the table. The buffet table is being employed more often to facilitate simple, efficient service for breakfast, luncheon, dinner, or cocktail hour, when service must be fast. Large numbers of guests can be taken care of quickly and with ease. An American table setting is used for buffet service, with fresh utensils set for each course. Using separate tables for meat-carving and dessert speeds service. Food served on the buffet should be arranged according to color and contour; and different sized and shaped dishes, accented with creative lighting, should be used. Rechauds and bain-maries will keep food warm. Tiered tables are not only decorative, but functional for displaying foods behind one another. Linen should be neatly spread and the table completely covered to cloak the view of the legs and underside. Table shapes can vary, but consideration should be given to traffic flow, since some shapes could hinder service.

INVOLVING THE GUEST

Americans not only enjoy being part of an exciting restaurant environment, but they also like to participate in it. Personality-type restaurants use various techniques to include their guests in the food production or service.

Self-service is one technique. Areas in the restaurant can be set aside for self-service salad bars, dessert tables, or soup kettles. The guest enjoys the feeling of taking as much of an item as desired, while the size of the plate or bowl provided and the timing of the delivery of the next course (speed of service) creates a minimal control system for the operator.

Involving the guest can also take the form of actually cooking or fabricating an item in the dining room, or right in front of the guest. The roast prime rib of beef carving station at the Royal Orleans Hotel in

Figure 8.39.   Fondue Set for Melted Cheese and Chocolate.

Figure 8.40.   Fondue Set for Hot Oil.

New Orleans and the roasting crepe-maker used by the Magic Pan Corporation are two examples. Probably the most successful operation of this nature is Benihana of Tokyo, with its hibachi grill-table. The "chef" combines the skills of a samurai swordsman, waiter, chef, and toastmaster all in a single job description. This eliminates the need for a large kitchen and dining room staff, while providing the guest with highly styled but simple fare.

Fondue is another popular example of customer cookery. Fondue means "melt" — crusty bread is coated with melted cheese, or fresh fruit, squares of cake, and marshmallows are dipped into melted chocolate. Special fondue sets are used, composed of a heating element, a container for the melted cheese or chocolate, and long spears for dipping.

Fondue also refers to the practice of cooking bite-sized morsels of meat, poultry, seafood, or vegetables in hot oil. The cooked tidbits are generally dipped into accompanying sauces which have been placed on the table. The container for the hot oil is usually higher than that used for the cheese or chocolate melt. The higher sides prevent the hot oil from splattering onto the guest.

Guest involvement has become a rapidly growing form of merchandising. As the use of convenience foods at home increases, more people derive excitement and pleasure from active participation in restaurants, without the bother of preparation or cleanup.

PROMOTIONS

Specials — also known as chef's suggestions or house specialties — are excellent ways to promote sales. These promotional offerings need not be less expensive than regular menu items but can be seasonal, exotic, innovative, or provocative dishes designed to give the guest a break from the ordinary. Extra time and care in the handling and promoting of these items can constitute an above average profit. The following are some suggestions for direct merchandising.

Menu clip-ons: Take care not to cover any printed portion of the menu.

Table tents: Tents are excellent for daily, weekly, or seasonal special promotions, and they eliminate the need for menu additions.

Chalkboards: A newly-popular merchandising technique, chalkboards are easily changeable from day to day.

Verbal comments: Direct announcements by the waiter of daily and house specials can greatly increase sales.

For two or more: Menu items priced especially for multiple orders can simplify the ordering process for both guest and waiter, even while conveying the impression that the dish is extra special.

SECONDARY PRODUCT LINES

The primary products are those items which patrons expect to purchase in a restaurant — the food and beverages to be consumed within the establishment. Generally the primary product line is the bill of fare as

Figure 8.41. Fondue at Swiss Hutte, O'Hare Hilton.

Figure 8.42. Benihana Robata at the Las Vegas Hilton.

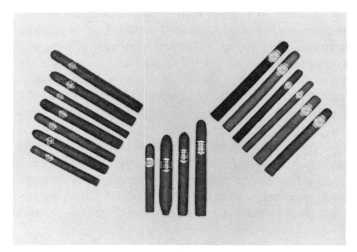

Figure 8.43. Cigars Sold at "21" Club, New York City.

Figure 8.44. Tobacco Counter at "21" Club, New York City.

Figure 8.45. Tobacco Counter at Windows on the World, New York City.

offered on the menu, wine list, and dessert card. It is the line of products which the guest is obviously going to buy.

The secondary product line is made up of sellable items like cigarettes; regular and house brand cigars; specialty glassware in which drinks are served; canned or jarred goods like salad dressings, sauces, and pickled items; baked goods; sweets; and exotic foods which might not be readily available in the geographical area. Secondary sales and the counters or displays which promote them should blend in with the type and style of restaurant. The retail sales of these products are a source of extra income and involve a minimum amount of work once the product line has been established. All house-brand products should bear the name, logo, and location of the operation. This will prove to be an additional source of advertising.

9
GUEST CHECK WRITING AND MONEY HANDLING

The guest check is the most important business form used in a restaurant for controlling food and beverage. It serves three specific purposes: first, to order food from the kitchen and/or drinks from the bar; second, to obtain payment from the guest; and third, to account to the cost control department for items sold.

All information concerning a sales transaction between server and patron must be recorded on the guest check. To organize this data, most guest checks are made up of three distinct parts: an information box, the body of the guest check, and the customer's receipt stub.

The information box contains data of a statistical nature such as the date, table number, and server. It might also include such items as the number of guests at the table; the location of the table, if there is more than one dining area; what time the order was taken and served; and the sequential number of the guest check. The sequential number must appear on the customer's receipt as well. Some guest check designs bear the check number on the body of the check instead of on the information stub. This data is used by the server at the time of service to assure that tables are receiving the proper order. Management also uses these facts to compile information such as how many tables or covers were served on a given day; how many meals; how many tables and meals were served by each server. Recorded ordering and serving times will allow management to identify busy periods and to adjust service or kitchen staff to meet the demand. The sequential guest check numbers provide a control system for management by which every order is paid or accounted for.

The body of the guest check includes what is ordered; how it is to be prepared; special or specific requirements for the food ordered; the amount charged for each item; the total charged for all items; taxes charged; and the service charge, if applicable.

The receipt stub will be offered to the guest at the completion of the meal. It should include the name of the operation; the logo, if there is one; the date of the transaction; the total amount of the bill; and the sequential guest check number.

The composition of guest checks will vary considerably. The nature and style of an operation will help to dictate the type of guest check used. Reliability restaurants that maintain a California-style menu may have the name and price of the items imprinted on the guest check to simplify order taking. Some guest checks will include an area for tallying the orders by courses — for listing how many and which appetizers, entrees, or salad dressings were ordered.

Guest checks are issued by management to the designated cashier, who is responsible for signing them

Escoffier Room

CHECK NO.
283779

APTZ.	ENTREE	SALAD	BEV.	
PATE	TROUT	V+O		17.50
H'DV	LAMB CHOP Ⓡ	RUS		18.75
PATE	SIRLOIN ⓂⓇ	ITAL		19.50

2 PATE	1 TROUT		1 Russian
1 hors d'oeuvre	1 LAMB CHOP Ⓡ		1 ITALIAN
	1 SIRLOIN ⓂⓇ		1 V+O

ORDER TAKEN 8:05	ORDER SERVED 8:40	FOOD	55.75
		BAR	27.45
TABLE NO. 12 DATE 8/7		SUB TOTAL	83.20
		+ TAX	6.65
SERVED BY Patrick		TOTAL DUE	89.85
PAID BY cash			

Date	No. Persons	Amount	Check No.
8/7	3	89.85	283779
Receipt			

Escoffier Room

Figure 9.1. Completed Guest Check.

out to the waiters at the beginning of each shift and for collecting all unused checks at the end of each shift. Before and after each meal period, the sequential numbers should be inspected to make certain that all checks which have been signed for are in the properly numbered sequence.

WRITING AN ORDER

The check should be legibly and clearly written so that it can be interpreted by the person taking the order, by the guest, the kitchen staff, the cashier, the auditor, and by another waiter who might have to take over the table or replace someone at the end of the shift. Symbols and abbreviations for food and beverage items will vary depending on the operation. All staff within an operation should attempt to use the same set of abbreviations, to avoid confusion. Management will often adopt standard abbreviations to be used by all service staff.

Generally, one check is written for the entire table, unless separate checks are requested when the order is taken. To facilitate writing and interpreting the guest check, a chair-numbering system is often developed by management and used by all members of the serving staff. Usually the seat closest to the entrance is seat number one on each table. Proceeding clockwise, each seat is numbered consecutively. If some places at a table are empty, those that are occupied retain their original chair number. Noting the order by seat number will allow the waiter to know what each guest has ordered. When the food arrives, the waiter can serve the appropriate food to each guest. This lends a professional touch to the service. Theoretically, when the order is taken according to seat number, any waiter — even one who did not take the order — will be able to serve the correct food to each guest by simply consulting the guest check.

All data in the information box should be filled in before you approach the table. Then approach the table unobtrusively and ask in a pleasant voice, "Are you ready to order?" or "May I take your order?" Whenever possible, orders are taken from the guest's right side. Traditionally, ladies' and older persons' orders are taken first and placed alongside their corresponding seat number on the check. Next, the gentlemen's orders are taken. Finally the host, if known, will order last.

Note the food ordered in the sequence that it will be served, and take the complete order all at once. Take each person's appetizer, soup, salad, and entree order in that sequence before moving onto the next person. Of course, if salad is to be served after the entree, take the salad order after the entree order. It is advisable to repeat each order to the guest as you record it, to make sure that the information is being interpreted correctly.

After retreating from the table, the waiter tallies the order in the space provided on the guest check, or on a separate duplicate check known as a "dupe." Tallies are usually done by course. Separate dupes may be required

Escoffier Room

CHECK NO. 283779

APTZ.	ENTREE	SALAD	BEV.	
ESCAR	SCALLOP	ITAL		22.75
ESCAR	CORNISH HEN	RUS		19.25
PATE	SIRLOIN (R)	ITAL		(13.75)
SHRIMP	PORK LOIN	V&O		16.50
				17.50
	VOID WRONG RING			

2 Escargot	1 SCALLOP	2 ITALIAN
1 PATE	1 CORNISH HEN	1 Russian
1 SHRIMP	1 SIRLOIN (R)	1 V&O
	1 PORK LOIN	

ORDER TAKEN 6:30	ORDER SERVED 7:15	FOOD	76.00
TABLE NO. 14	DATE 8/10	BAR	32.65
		SUB TOTAL	108.65
SERVED BY Lorraine		+ TAX	8.69
PAID BY Am. Exp.		TOTAL DUE	117.34

Date 8/10	No. Persons 4	Amount 117.34	Check No. 283779

Receipt

Escoffier Room

Figure 9.2. Voiding Errors.

for the appetizer and salad if these items are picked up from separate stations in the kitchen. The design of the guest check may include the necessary dupes in the form of tear-away carbon copies of the original guest check. Dupes are often color coded, with a different color assigned to each station.

Depending on the control system used at a particular operation, guest checks can have any number of dupes. There is usually a minimum of three: one apiece for the kitchen, waiter, and guest. The kitchen will use a dupe to fill food orders. The waiter will use his copy to know to whom each order belongs. The guest's copy will be used as the bill and later be turned over to the cashier.

If a precheck system is used, dollar amounts will be rung up on the register before a dupe can go into the kitchen. This is to insure that all food orderd from the kitchen is charged to the guest. Should an error be made after an item is rung up, there is usually a prescribed house policy on the handling of a void or miss-ring. Generally, the course of action includes the following:

1. Circle the dollar amount and draw a line to a blank space in the body of the check. Never erase or black out an incorrect item.
2. Give a brief explanation of why the item was voided.
3. Register the new amount on the check, on a new line.
4. Have the cashier or manager designated to handle voids initial the transaction. A tally sheet for all voids is often used to simplify the reconciliation of voids on all checks.
5. If, for whatever reason, the whole check is voided, draw a line through the entire check and indicate the fact that it was voided and the reasons.

If an entire check has been filled and a second check is required, the first one should be subtotaled and added to the second check. When presenting the check to the guest for payment, both checks should be included.

CHECK PRESENTATION AND PAYMENT

After the meal is over and everyone appears to be finished, it is permissible to ask, "Would you care for anything else?" If the response is negative, a waiter may ask, "May I bring you your check?" Never tally the check before you ask permission, as it looks like you are anxious to get rid of the guests. Before the final tally, questionable prices should be checked against the menu or wine list. Check the subtotal twice. If it does not add up to the same amount, check it again. Next the sales tax must be computed. The percent of tax will

```
ST-II0.7 (5/71)
N.Y. State Department of Taxation and Finance - Sales Tax Bureau
```

7% SALES AND USE TAX COLLECTION CHART **7%**
Effective June 1, 1971

Amount of Sale	Tax to be Collected	Amount of Sale	Tax to be Collected
$0.01 to $0.10	None	$5.08 to $5.21	$.36
.11 to .20	1¢	5.22 to 5.35	.37
.21 to .33	2¢	5.36 to 5.49	.38
.34 to .47	3¢	5.50 to 5.64	.39
.48 to .62	4¢	5.65 to 5.78	.40
.63 to .76	5¢	5.79 to 5.92	.41
.77 to .91	6¢	5.93 to 6.07	.42
.92 to 1.07	7¢	6.08 to 6.21	.43
1.08 to 1.21	8¢	6.22 to 6.35	.44
1 22 to 1.35	9¢	6.36 to 6.49	.45
1.36 to 1.49	$.10	6.50 to 6.64	.46
1.50 to 1.64	.11	6.65 to 6.78	.47
1.65 to 1.78	.12	6.79 to 6.92	.48
1.79 to 1.92	.13	6.93 to 7.07	.49
1.93 to 2.07	.14	7.08 to 7.21	.50
2.08 to 2.21	.15	7.22 to 7.35	.51
2.22 to 2.35	.16	7.36 to 7.49	.52
2.36 to 2.49	.17	7.50 to 7.64	.53
2.50 to 2.64	.18	7.65 to 7.78	.54
2.65 to 2.78	.19	7.79 to 7.92	.55
2.79 to 2.92	.20	7.93 to 8.07	.56
2.93 to 3.07	.21	8.08 to 8.21	.57
3.08 to 3.21	.22	8.22 to 8.35	.58
3.22 to 3.35	.23	8.36 to 8.49	.59
3.36 to 3.49	.24	8.50 to 8.64	.60
3.50 to 3.64	.25	8.65 to 8.78	.61
3.65 to 3.78	.26	8.79 to 8.92	.62
3.79 to 3.92	.27	8.93 to 9.07	.63
3.93 to 4.07	.28	9.08 to 9.21	.64
4.08 to 4.21	.29	9.22 to 9.35	.65
4.22 to 4.35	.30	9.36 to 9.49	.66
4.36 to 4.49	.31	9.50 to 9.64	.67
4.50 to 4.64	.32	9.65 to 9.78	.68
4.65 to 4.78	.33	9.79 to 9.92	.69
4.79 to 4.92	.34	9.93 to 10.00	.70
4.93 to 5.07	.35		

On sales over $10.00, compute the tax by multiplying the amount of sale by the applicable tax rate and rounding the result to the nearest whole cent.

Figure 9.3. Tax Chart.

vary from state to state, county to county, and city to city. For accuracy and consistency, use a tax chart whenever possible. Compute and record the service charge if applicable. Finally, calculate the grand total.

The guest check may be presented in a special book turned face down in a simply folded napkin on a plate, or folded in half on a cash tray. If no one at the table has indicated that they, specifically, want the check or that they are hosting the party, it is best to place the check in a neutral zone not too close to anyone. If there is an argument about who is going to pay, again place it in a neutral zone and remove yourself from the situation. Be prompt, but not overbearing in retrieving the money once it is placed on the plate. After the money has been placed on the plate, return to the table and discreetly count the money. Write the total amount received on the check. This procedure will protect you from possible errors in handling the cash, or from a guest who has forgotten the amount of money he paid.

Present the guest check and cash to the cashier, double check the change, and complete the receipt. Return the plate to the table with a smile and a thank you. Never hover over the table waiting for the gratuity.

If the guest has any questions concerning the bill, answer them politely, as it is the right of the guest to understand exactly what all charges represent. If an error has been made, the check should be refigured and presented again. Should the guest become difficult, turn the problem over to a member of management.

Personal Checks

If the management accepts personal checks, there should be a prescribed procedure to follow. This procedure will usually include, but not be limited to, the following steps:

1. Check the date written on the check.
2. Compare the numerical figure with the written dollar amount.
3. Be sure the check is made directly to the restaurant. It is not advisable to accept second party checks.
4. Request and record identification of some sort — a current driver's license, a valid credit card, or a check cashing card will usually suffice. If the dollar amount is above a maximum established by management, two pieces of identification and approval are standard procedure.
5. Initial the check and present it with the guest check to the cashier.

Traveler's Checks

In most cases, traveler's checks are as good as cash. Certain precautions should be taken, however, when accepting traveler's checks as payment:

1. Make sure that traveler's checks are made payable to the restaurant and not left blank.
2. Remember that the second signature must be written in your presence or in the presence of the person cashing the check.
3. Compare the counter signature with the original. If it is the same signature, handle the payment as a cash transaction.
4. If counter signature is not clearly the same as the original, you may request that the name be written again on the back of the check.

Credit Card Transactions

Credit cards are widely used in the U.S. A recent report suggested that, if the economy remains strong enough, credit cards may eventually replace coin and paper money as we know it today. Most operations subscribe to one or two major credit card companies like American Express or Master Charge for the convenience of their patrons. The seals of those credit cards honored by the establishment are generally displayed near the front door, by the cashier, and sometimes on the menu. If the guest chooses to pay with a credit card, carry out the following steps to complete the transaction:

1. Take the credit card and the guest check to the cashier, who will imprint the card and the date on a form called a "charge record."
2. Fill in the charges and the tax.
3. Present the charge record and a pen to the guest, who will add the gratuity (unless he wishes to leave cash), tabulate the total charges, and sign the charge record.
4. Compare the signature on the charge record with the signature on the card.
5. Check the card number against the listings in the credit card cancellation bulletin.
6. Return the credit card and the customer's copy of the charge record to the patron.

If the guest's credit card number is listed in the cancellation bulletin, call the designated credit card authorization number and ask for instructions on how to proceed with the transaction. Other circumstances that may warrant calling for authorization: if charges are above the floor limit established for your operation by the credit card company; if the signature on the card and the charge record do not compare properly; if the card appears to be tampered with physically; if the valid date on the card has not yet passed; or if the card has expired. When authorization has been granted, many credit card companies require that an approval code number be recorded on the charge record. Registering this code number protects you from loss due to fraudulent use of the credit card by the patron.

Vouchers

Complimentary meals or vouchers are usually handled with a special letter or a form known as a "chit." The chit or letter should be filled out and correctly verified. It should be signed and turned in with the guest check.

| ABC Restaurant |
| Good For One Cover - Food and Non-Alcoholic Beverages Only |

☐ LUNCHEON   ☐ DINNER

Date _____

Authorized By _____
                        signature

Authorized To _____
                        signature

No Cash Value - Maximum not to exceed $10.00
Not Transferable

Figure 9.4. Chit or Voucher.

A notation should be made on the guest check that a chit or letter was used. If the dollar amount of the charges exceeds the allotted figure, the difference must be paid in cash.

SPECIAL PROBLEMS

Money awareness is extremely important at all times. Unfortunately, not everyone is honest. The best safeguard against dishonesty is concentration. Anyone handling money must be careful to execute each step of a transaction separately.

1. Count the cash received from the guest.
2. Mark the amount on the guest check.
3. Count the change before it is returned to the guest.
4. When checking the change, do not add or subtract. Rather, count from the amount owed to the amount paid.
5. To avoid confusion, handle one transaction at a time, so that there is no question about the moneys owed and returned.

These basic rules will help guard against short-change artists or anyone who is trying to take advantage of you for their profit.

A "walk out" is a guest who leaves the restaurant without paying his bill. If you notice a patron leaving, assume that they have forgotten and tactfully remind them, out of earshot of the other guests, about the guest check. Always notify management immediately if a guest leaves the premises without paying. Let management determine whether to call the police. Do not try to apprehend the guest yourself, as this could be dangerous.

If a guest is without money, checks, or credit cards and has no obvious means of paying his tab, it is best to notify the manager or supervisor immediately. They should have a prescribed technique for handling the situation which does not involve the server. The decision to call the police should be made by them.

The most important thing to remember during a robbery is to stay calm. Avoid direct eye contact, as this can intimidate and anger a robber. Heroic or dramatic actions can endanger your life and the lives of others. It is more important to try to remember any physical details about the thief that will help to identify him later.

GRATUITIES

Tipping is said to have originated from the practice of giving an innkeeper a gratuity in return for keeping one's stay a secret. It evolved into the custom of paying a little extra in advance for proper and prompt service. In fact, the word "tip" is believed to have derived from the acronym of the words "To Insure Promptness," and the plural, "tips," from "To Insure Proper Service." The practice of tipping restaurant service personnel has developed to the point where gratuities are expected, and form the largest part of a person's wage. Self-service restaurants have become popular not only because they provide quick service and standardized foods, but also because tipping is not required.

Tipping can be an awkward situation for the guest, as well as for the server. Often guests do not know how much to tip, and feel foolish trying to figure out a customary percentage of the bill to arrive at a suitable figure. The server is often anxious about the gratuity, fearing that it will be inadequate or even nonexistent.

To help alleviate this uncomfortable situation, many operations are adding a service charge directly to the guest check. Usually an addition of 15 percent to 22 percent of the cost of food and beverage can be imposed by the house to insure the income of the service person and make it easier for the guest to tip. Trends indicate that this practice may eventually be the norm, rather than the exception to the rule. To succesfully implement the service charge, it must first be properly sold to the public. The patron should be informed via the menu or a table tent that a service charge will be added to the final bill, so that there is no surprise when the check is received. A service charge does not necessarily mean a waiter will lose his competitive spirit and provide lackluster service. Often cash tips will be left along with the service charge if the service is exceptional.

Another contemporary approach to tipping is for the restaurant operator to establish proper salaries for professional service personnel, building the added expense into the sale price of the meal. In this way the operator assumes financial responsibility for the service staff.

Initiating a service charge or establishing suitable salary scales for dining room staff will help to instill a

DAILY RECORD OF TIPS

EMPLOYER'S NAME

MONTH | YEAR

Date	Tips	Date	Tips
1	$	17	$
2		18	
3		19	
4		20	
5		21	
6		22	
7		23	
8		24	
9		25	
10		26	
11		27	
12		28	
13		29	
14		30	
15		31	
16		Total $	

Form 4070A (1–66)

Figure 9.5. Daily Record of Tips.

Form 4070 (Jan. 1966) U.S. Treasury Department Internal Revenue Service	EMPLOYEE'S REPORT ON TIPS	Social Security Number
Employee's name and address		
Employer's name and address		
Month or shorter period in which tips were received from ...., 19......., to ...., 19.......		Amount $..............................
Signature		Date

Figure 9.6. Employee's Report of Tips.

more professional attitude in the waiter and, in the long run, will reduce the amount of dissatisfied customers. These practices also prompt restaurateurs to be more efficient in their planning, scheduling, and service techniques. Assuring the server of a livable wage would be one solution to the current lack of truly professional waiters.

Finally, it should be mentioned that it is the employee's responsibility to keep a record of and report all tips to the employer, who in turn passes the information on to the Internal Revenue Service. Cash tips must be reported to the employer on a monthly basis, on or before the tenth of the month following that in which the tips were received. To facilitate this procedure, tips can be recorded daily and tabulated on a monthly basis, using a Daily Record of Tips form or similar worksheet. Monthly reports of tips to the employer can be made by using an Employee's Report of Tips form. Both are U.S. Treasury Department Internal Revenue Service forms. Willful neglect by an employee to report tip income to an employer can result in a penalty of 50% of the tax due on unreported tips.

10 BANQUETS

BANQUETS

A banquet is an elaborate and often ceremonial meal for many people, frequently in honor of a person, persons, or an occasion. In his *Physiology of Taste*, Brillat-Savarin established the rules of harmonious dining for great and gala dinners.

"Let the dining room be more than amply lighted, the linen of dazzling cleanliness, and the temperature maintained at from sixty to sixty-eight degrees fahrenheit;

"Let the gentlemen be witty without pretension, and the ladies charming without too much coquetry;

"Let the dishes be of exquisite quality, but limited in their number, and the wines of the first rank also, each according to its degree;

"Let the progression of the former be from the most substantial to the lightest, and of the latter from the simplest wines to the headiest;

"Let the tempo of eating be moderate, the dinner being the last affair of the day; the guests should behave like travelers who must arrive together at the same destination;

"Let the coffee be piping hot, and the liquers of the host's especial choice...."

All of the factors which Brillat-Savarin has listed — lighting, linen, wine selection, menu composition, pace — are items which can be planned for; and with proper planning the affair can be executed to perfection. This planning and execution is the job of the dining room personnel.

There are essentially three types of catering businesses: an establishment which does catering exclusively; a restaurant with full catering facilities; and a restaurant with limited catering facilities. Throughout the chapter we will refer to catering and banquets mainly as they pertain to restaurants.

ADVANTAGES OF CATERING

In catering, all sales are booked in advance. Consequently, the number of guests and the food to be served are all known before-hand. This results in some distinct advantages:

Cash deposit, and so an assured amount of working capital

Excellent portion and cost control

Controlled labor costs with a set number of hours and employees required for a function

Small inventory costs (Specialty items can be rented and costs passed on to the client.)

Accurately forecasted sales and profits

THE BANQUET MANAGER

The organizer of a banquet responds directly to the needs of a specific market. Banquet sales are used to generate additional income, thereby increasing the productivity of an operation. When sales are great enough, a special banquet manager is employed to:

Schedule the affair.

Develop and sell food and beverage menus.

Develop and sell such extra services as flowers, photographs, music, and special effects.

Organize the function for the kitchen and service staff.

Accommodate and execute special requests.

Be on duty to insure that the affair runs smoothly.

Coordinate the sales force, cooking staff, and service personnel.

The management of a catering operation requires a complete knowledge of foodservice managerial skills. The three main areas of concern and emphasis in successful catering and banqueting are: financial control of the operations; coordination of staffing; and the development of menus and services within the limits established by costing and pricing guidelines.

Careful prior planning prevents poor performance. This is the key to successful banqueting. Controls are best administered in the form of detailed checklists. These lists itemize all of the ingredients necessary to present the product in the desired manner. Checklists solve problems before they occur by informing all concerned employees of the pertinent details of a function.

BOOKING A FUNCTION

It is advisable to follow certain procedures in booking, planning, and executing a banquet. Adherence to these procedures will assure that optimum controls are maintained throughout all stages of the affair, and will provide a vehicle for the step-by-step organization of the function.

Inquiry: Most inquiries are made on the phone. Request the potential customer to come in to the restaurant to discuss the affair. This will increase the chance of booking the function and aid in selling the products and services offered.

Estimate: Include on all estimates the date of the affair; number of people; type of service; cost per person; what is to be provided for that cost; and any extras which might be needed, such as attendants, bartenders, or flowers. If a tentative booking is made at this time, enter it into the Master Banquet Book immediately so that other bookings will not be duplicated. The Master Banquet Book is a record of all tentative and confirmed functions, giving the dates and locations of each affair. A file folder should be started when the booking is entered, to organize all correspondence and information concerning the affair. Keep track of the number of estimates given out against the number of bookings. If the client decides not to confirm the booking, gracefully attempt to find out why. If the client agrees with the estimate, require a signed letter of confirmation.

Letter of confirmation: This document must be signed by the client and the agent. It is a legal contract. A deposit generally accompanies the confirmation, the amount varying depending on house policy. A receipt is in order. Once a function has been confirmed, the tentative entry in the Master Banquet Book should be changed accordingly.

Contract: One month prior to the function, a formal contract should be signed and accompanied by another deposit. All the specifics of the affair must be spelled out and agreed upon. No details should be assumed by either party. A signed contract will protect both parties from any misunderstanding. The contract must be signed by the client and by the catering manager or other authorized persons. In the event of a cancellation, house policy will dictate the disposition of the deposit. It can be returned in full or in part, depending on the term of the contract.

Floor plan: Draw up a floor plan at this time. Copies should be distributed to all departments concerned.

Function sheet: The function sheet, also known as the work order, is a duplicate of the contract without the prices. The function sheet will serve as the basis for ordering food and staffing the affair.

Finalizing the details: No later than one week prior to the affair, the client and management should meet to finalize all aspects of the function.

Purchasing and renting: All necessary food items can be purchased and needed equipment rented for the affair.

Work schedules: From the function sheet, establish work schedules and distribute them to all departments involved — accounting, kitchen, front of the house, stewarding, and any others.

Party: Prior to the party, all personnel must be informed of their responsibilities in level meetings. The person in charge is authorized to take a final count of the guests, and to itemize and tabulate any services or products provided which were not covered in the contract. Ideally, these extras should not be authorized without the client's signature.

Final bill: The final bill should be paid at the time specified in the contract. Some state tax regulations require that the bill be kept on file for up to seven years, as with other financial documents.

Follow-up: A verbal or written follow-up should always be made. This will promote goodwill between the operator and client, and provide a basis for performance evaluation. Negative feedback will point out areas which need improvement; positive feedback will highlight strong points. A monthly form detailing all catering business is another important tool in evaluating the effectiveness of the catering department. It will break down the total income into categories for analysis and future budgeting.

Filing: Establish some kind of filing system which will assure the use of past affairs as a source of future business. An active file might contain such affairs such as annual parties, which can generate return business.

BANQUET SERVICE

A banquet uses table service variations: American, French, Russian, or buffet service. All types require elaborate planning to ensure success. If there are to be variations of established service procedures, these changes should be organized well before the affair. All service personnel should be duly informed of any changes or variations prior to the affair. Therefore, the demands put upon catering personnel require a total understanding of all details of a function, and the mastery of a variety of styles of service.

To ensure that all duties are covered and that everyone is aware of their responsibilities, a meeting should be held prior to the affair. The head waiter should take this time to remind all personnel that, although a routine function for themselves, the banquet is a rare event for the guests, and every effort should be made to make it a special one. Particular points to be covered prior to the function are:

Number of covers per waiter, per wine waiter, per busperson

Table plan

Mise en Place, with attention to special equipment

Specific points to remember, such as speciality presentations or styles of service

Sequence of service for a food, beverage, and entertainment

STAFFING AND SETTING UP FOR A BANQUET

The number of service personnel needed for a banquet will depend on the total number of guests and the style of service. If American service is used at the banquet, allow one waiter per twenty guests. For French and Russian service figure two waiters per thirty guests and, for a buffet, schedule one waiter for every thirty guests.

An open bar means that guests drink as much as they like in a certain time period. No guest is charged for drinks, but the host makes payment in the prearranged fashion. At a cash bar, each guest pays for each drink as it is ordered. Generally at a banquet one bartender is assigned for every fifty people on an open or cash bar. For cocktail receptions or for butler service of hors d'oeuvres, one waiter is scheduled for each thirty to forty guests.

When setting up the dining room, the head table should be positioned for optimum viewing by all guests. Use a dais or raised platform if necessary, to eliminate the problems of viewing the head table. The remaining table plan will depend on the type of function, the size and shape of the room, the number of guests to be seated, and the preferences of the organizer.

Figure 10.1. Banquet Seating at Peachtree Plaza, Atlanta.

Round tables are ideal for banquets, as they allow for easy conversation between guests. Square footage allotments for banquets will vary depending on the specific service details. For sit-down affairs it is recommended to allow from twelve to fifteen square feet per person; for buffet service allow ten to twelve square feet per person.

All tables with the exception of the head table should be numbered. Table numbers can be mounted on stands and made visible to guests from the entrance of the room. Guests can obtain their table numbers from either a master seating chart or a special table set up to supply table numbers. The seating chart should be drawn prior to the affair. The organizer will be able to refer to the seating chart for checking all necessary arrangements and for stationing waiters. The host will consult the seating chart in developing a guest-seating plan. Any seating plan should allow for extra guests. A minimum of 10 percent of the total number of guests should be adequate, but it is best to discuss this with the host.

Tablecloths should be laid in an organized and systematic manner. Any overlap of cloths on a table should face away from the main entrance so that it will be less visible to guests viewing the room on arrival. First impressions are very important. Tableware will be determined by the menu. All tableware should be laid according to the style and sequence of service as outlined in chapter 6 — *Service.*

Figure 10.2. Table Markers.

RUSSIAN SERVICE

The main goal of Russian service is to serve fully cooked food while it is still hot and to serve it in a tasteful manner. It is particularly useful at banquets, or wherever large groups of people must be quickly served. All food is fully cooked, placed on platters, and garnished in the kitchen. The platters are brought to the dining room by a waiter, who presents the platter to the head of the table and shows it to the guests before beginning to serve. The waiter stands with feet together, to the left of the guest. The platter rests on the palm of the left hand, which is protected by a folded side towel. The waiter bends at the waist, advancing the left foot slightly and bringing the platter close to the rim of the guest's dinner plate. The food is plated with the aid of a serving spoon and fork in the waiter's right hand.

Considerable skill and dexterity are required to perform proper Russian service. Trays can be hot and heavy and must be held firmly in the left hand while the food is being served with the right. Practice is required to prevent dropping and breaking the food or spilling the sauce. Precise timing and organization are essential if the food is to reach the guest at its peak. The personnel in the kitchen must calculate the exact moment to platter the food so that it is presented to the guest without any change in flavor. Carving must be done in a minimum amount of time. Coordination for plating and serving throughout the meal can only be achieved if there are open and free-flowing lines of communication between the kitchen and the dining room.

While speed of service is essential, the food must still be arranged attractively and correctly. This is especially true when the dishes are accompanied by

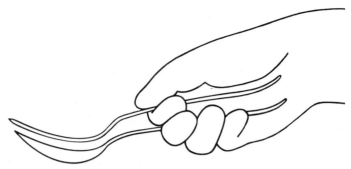

Figure 10.3. Fork and Spoon Held in Right Hand for Russian Service.

different garnishes, which must blend perfectly with the principal ingredient. The entree is placed on the lower portion of the guest's plate, and the accompaniments placed neatly above the entree. These items should be arranged on the guest's plate in the same form and shape as they appear on the platter. Handle the food as little as possible to avoid breaking and changing its appearance.

Some additional suggestions for successful Russian service are:

Know the number of portions expected from each platter.

Use a clean serving spoon and fork for each dish.

If a food item, such as a puree, sticks to the spoon and fork, use a separate set of flatware for that item.

Lift and place the food gracefully. Never slide it onto the guest's plate.

11
RESERVATIONS

A reservation is a recorded promise or guarantee of a table in a restaurant. House policy will dictate whether or not reservations will be taken. Some restaurants pride themselves on long lines of guests who wait for their tables. Other establishments boast of how far in advance their reservation book is filled.

The world famous Galatoire's on Bourbon Street in New Orleans chooses not to accept reservations. Guests wait in line while the first come, first served technique of seating is used. Since this is established house policy, the guest knows in advance that there may be a wait. This type of seating policy maximizes the use of all tables as they become available. There are never any empty tables waiting for a party to arrive at a designated time.

Restaurants that do accept reservations employ one of two approaches in seating — continuous seating at anytime during the meal period, or established seating times at intervals in the meal period. Before a decision is made as to the type of seating, the length of time it takes to dine must be estimated. This is done by tabulating the number of minutes it will take for each course to be served and consumed.

Some factors which influence the length of the meal are lighting, music, movement of the staff, style of service, and the mood set by the ambience. Brighter lighting, faster music, and quicker service will usually, but not always, make the diner eat more quickly. Conversely, dimmer lighting, slower music, and a gracious movement of the service staff will set a more leisurely pace.

Continuous seating is recommended for shorter meals. Reservations should be booked at fifteen to thirty minute intervals, however, to avoid overloading a station or the kitchen with orders all coming in at one time. This will help to develop a smooth flow in order taking and to synchronize the output of the kitchen. Usually, the shorter the meal, the faster the turnover and the lower the check average.

Seating at established meal times is recommended for longer meals. Reservations should be taken for one or two specific times — a first seating at 6:30 PM, for example, and a second at 8:30 PM. A slower paced meal will result in less turnover and, usually, a higher check average.

TAKING A RESERVATION

Telephone courtesy is a must in taking reservations. The information necessary for the proper reservation must be taken in an organized but not a mechanical manner. Here are some guidelines for taking reservations:

Start with an appropriate greeting: "Good morning," "Good afternoon," or "Good evening."

Note the name of the party.

Request the date of the reservation. If the date is booked, offer an alternate date. If all tables are booked for an evening and the client is adamant about coming on that particular evening, he might be placed on a waiting list. Usually no more than four parties are held on the waiting list. They will call or be called on the day of the tentative reservation for confirmation or rejection.

Request the time. If the time is booked, again offer an alternative. The policy on holding reservations might be explained at this point in the conversation. It might be suggested that the party arrive early.

Request the party's telephone number. This should be taken for two reasons: to reconfirm with the guest on the day of the reservation; and so that they can be reached, should unexpected problems arise.

Note the number of guests in the party and any special considerations: high chair, wheelchair, flowers, birthday cakes, special occasion, or champagne.

The initials of the person taking the reservation might be included in case there are questions or problems concerning arrangements. The manager or maitre d' may make additions or corrections to the original arrangements which might contradict house policy. These changes should be noted and initialed.

The date on which the reservation was taken may also be included. This is to protect the house should any question arise about the reservation. This bit of information will also let management know how far in advance reservations are being requested.

When a large group wishes to dine, several suggestions might improve the quality of their meal:

Recommend that the group arrive early, before the bulk of the business starts.

Try to establish a set menu for the group. Mail to the person in charge several menus from which to choose, or create a set dinner. Set menus make it easier for the kitchen to handle a large party and ensure faster service in the dining room.

Arrange the wine selection in advance.

Before their arrival, establish a plan for handling gratuities and payment of the check.

To create good feeling in the host who has reserved a table, be it for two or twenty, a "reserved" card can be placed on the assigned table prior to the guests' arrival. Printing the host's name on the "reserved" card makes the party feel especially important. Some operations go to the expense of imprinting matchbooks with the name of the party and setting them on the table.

It is advisable to keep the number of persons authorized to take reservations to a minimum. This will limit the chance for errors and confusion. Ideally, it is best to assign to one person per shift the responsibility of taking reservations. This person should keep the reservation book close by so that he can refer to it directly. This practice will avoid overbookings and lost reservations. In the event that an unauthorizd person is the only one available to take a reservation, the name and telephone number of the party should be noted and turned over to the authorized person, who will follow up the request.

Reservations are generally recorded first on a telephone reservation form, or directly into the reservation

Figure 11.1. Reservation Desk. Top Shelf: Reservation Book, Telephone, Menu, Wine List, Pen. Middle Shelf: Telephone Answering Machine, Guest Checks. Bottom Shelf: Log Book, Phone Number File.

DATE *Nov. 15, 1979*

NAME	PHONE	COVERS	SPECIAL INSTRUCTIONS	TIME	TABLE NO.	DATE/INIT.
Addams, Mrs. M.	201-331-6244	6	champagne bucket	6:30	25	9/4 KD
Moore, Alison	516-769-4166	2		6:30	15	9/4 KD
Dubois, Jeanne	914-607-4711	3	birthday cake: Anne	7:00	16	9/5 KD
Harrison, George	201-671-1121	2		7:30	21	9/6 ZP
Stewart, Peter	518-843-2348	4		7:00	23	9/7 KD
Hampton, John	201-471-7893	5	anniversary party	6:30	14	9/7 KD
Cannoli, Maria	914-473-3812	2	birthday cake	6:30	12	9/7 ZP
Reuben, Sidney	201-333-2112	2	wheelchair	8:00	11	9/8 KD
Fitzgerald, Kathleen	518-876-7401	5		8:00	24	9/9 KD
Morrison, James	914-452-2810	4		7:30	22	9/9 KD

Figure 11.2. Page of a Reservation Book.

RESERVATION

DATE: ....

NO. IN PARTY: .... ☐ LUNCH   ☐ DINNER

TIME OF RESERVATION: .... ☐ MEMBER ☐ NON-MEMBER

NAME: ....

LOCATION: .... Telephone Number: ....

DATE TAKEN: ....

LOGGED BY: .... BY: ....

TIME TAKEN: **A.M.**—(9-10) (10-11) (11-12)
(*circle one*)
P.M.—(12-1) (1-2) (2-3) (3-4) (4-5) (5-6) (6-7) (7-8) (8-9) (9-10)

DRESS CODE:
FREE PARKING:
COVER CHARGE FOR NON-MEMBERS AT LUNCH:

Figure 11.3. Telephone Reservation Form.

book. If a telephone reservation form is used, information can be compiled later in the reservation book. Copies of the telephone reservation form are generally made and kept with the reservation book at the check-in desk. When the guests check in, they are given a copy of their reservation, which they present to the head waiter or captain at the dining area where the guests are seated.

The guest-check-in desk is also known as the reservation desk. This is often the station where tele-phone reservations are taken. During service, the reservation book belongs at the guest-check-in desk, where it is controlled by the maitre d'hotel or person in charge of seating. As guests arrive a notation should be made in the reservation book. Cancelled reservations can be noted in the reservation book with the use of highlighting ink. This allows the reader to know on sight that a booking has been cancelled, permits easy reading, and gives a neat appearance. The reservation desk should also be equipped with such items as a telephone; pen or pencil; menu; wine list; guest checks; dupes; log book, a telephone-number file listing employee and various emergency phone numbers; and perhaps a telephone-answering machine for recording reservation requests when the restaurant is closed.

WORK STATIONS AND STAFFING

By accepting reservations, a restaurant can predetermine the amount of business expected on a given day or night. Establishments where reservations are "required" will be able to predict business more accurately than operations where reservations are merely "suggested." In either case, reservations will aid management in scheduling and assigning staff for both the dining room and the kitchen.

Before work stations can be established, certain preliminary steps must be taken:

Determine the number of guests to be served by a waiter or team of captain and waiters. In French and Russian Service, a team can generally handle from twelve to fourteen guests. In American Service, figure eighteen to twenty guests per waiter; and at banquets, assign one waiter to every twenty-eight or thirty guests.

Draw a floor plan of the dining room — a schematic representation of the table arrangements.

Number all tables in the dining room.

There are several systems for assigning table numbers. One approach is to divide the dining room into rows. All tables in the first row will bear the prefix 1, the tables in the second row the prefix 2, and so on. If there are four tables in the second row, they will be assigned, in order, numbers 21, 22, 23, and 24. Using this system, a waiter who is told to deliver something to table 43, will know to go to the third table in the fourth row. Whatever system is chosen, be sure it is logical. Many restaurants employing this or most other systems eliminate table number 13, in much the same way that hotels do not list floor number 13.

Once the workload of each waiter has been established, a floor plan drawn, and table numbers assigned, the dining room can be sectioned into stations. The number of stations will be determined by the amount of expected business. Meal periods that are more active (Saturday nights) may require smaller stations, since more demands will be placed on the team or individual

waiter. Tables should be grouped into an area so that the server can easily keep a close watch on all tables in his station.

Flexibility and convertability are very important in adapting the dining room to the needs of the reservation book. Some suggestions are:

Fifty percent of the tables should be deuces. This allows for a greater variety of table set-ups and configurations.

Round tables should only be used for banquet service or for special effect, since they cannot be pushed together to achieve different configurations.

Figure 11.4. Statler Table—Four-Top.

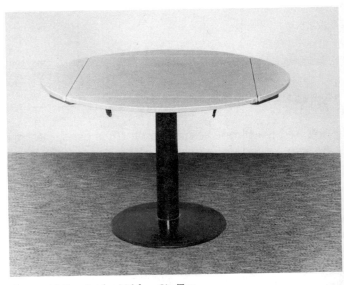

Figure 11.5. Statler Table—Six-Top.

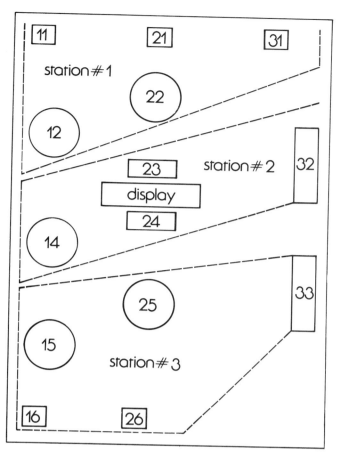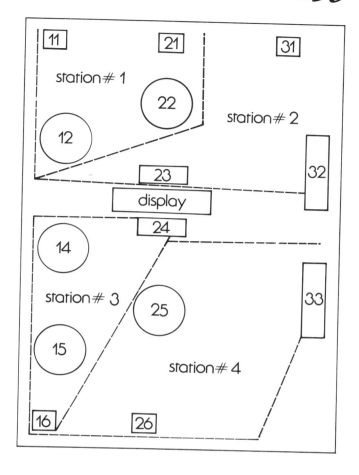

Figure 11.6. Floor Plan Sectioned into Three and Four Stations.

Try to avoid "moving lumber." Once the dining room is set for the evening, it can be rearranged slightly, but try to avoid moving tables into or out of the room. It is always distracting, even if the tables are collapsible.

Statler tables are an excellent way of converting square four tops to round six tops. Aisle clearance should be checked to establish the maximum usage for Statler tables. If too many are used at one time, service could be impaired by blocked aisles.

Double-check traffic and service aisles after placing tables into position. Be sure there is suitable access to the kitchen and adequate passage for carts or gueridons.

Once the dining room has been set up and work stations assigned, changes and adjustments can still be made. If four stations were assigned and business unexpectedly slows, the four stations can be cut back into three. Conversely, if a full complement of guests arrive unexpectedly, three stations can be converted into four, with the original staff splitting the fourth equally until more help arrives.

If service begins to suffer due to an unexpected increase in business, it is best to inform your guests of the problem early, to minimize complaints. There is no need for a lengthy explanation of circumstances. Merely inform the guests of the problem and the solution — additional help has been called in. Carry on as smoothly as possible.

Properly staffing a dining room takes time, patience, and access to certain facts. By recording daily information in a logbook, the recent traffic counts and even the previous year's counts for a given day can easily be checked. The logbook should record:

Number of guests served during each shift and for the day

Special events which may have had an effect on business

Weather conditions, such as inclement weather causing lateness or no shows

Maintenance problems

Station 1	2	4(6)	3(9)					
Station 2	4	2(6)	2(8)					
Station 3	3	4(7)						
Station 4	4	1(5)	3(8)					
Station 5	2	5(7)						

Figure 11.7.   Guest Seating Chart.

 Personnel or customer situations

 Any specific facts that might affect the traffic
 counts

This information will then be used when "guestimating" the number of staff required for a meal period.

SEATING THE GUESTS

Seating should be done evenly and methodically. Early in the shift, tables should not be filled at the same station in rapid succession. Proper reservation taking, of course, will help distribute the arrival times of patrons.

If a customer requests a table in a station out of sequence, explain that it has been previously reserved or is intended to accommodate special requests.

Whenever it is necessary to hold parties while their table is being set up or turned over, ask guests if they would like to wait in the bar. This will increase bar sales, temporarily divert their attention, and help them to relax. If they do not wish to drink, then the lobby or lounge area might be used for holding. Wherever it is that the guests wait, there should be regular communication between the maitre d' and the party. This will eliminate that feeling of being deserted.

Seating charts are used by the maitre d'hotel to distribute guests evenly over the dining room, and also to equalize the number of guests each server or team of servers is given in an evening. These charts should be kept in a dining room logbook. Insert the names of the servers next to the station number. This chart will also organize the rotation of stations. To be fair, stations should be rotated daily, since each station will be a different distance from the kitchen, have certain oddities, and be made up of varying table configurations such as all deuces. If a waiter is not practiced enough to handle a large or difficult station, the station should be divided or the waiter assigned to it on a slow evening. As the shift draws to a close, seating should be limited to one station or area so that guests are not scattered throughout the dining room. If this occurs and the surrounding guests depart, the remaining guests may feel uncomfortable and possibly stranded.

12
SALES AND CONTROLS

SALES

To sell is to influence or induce a patron to purchase an item or service. Dining room personnel must not only serve the guest, but also sell to the guest. Besides being a server, showman, and host, the waiter is also a salesman. An efficient and persuasive salesman will constantly strive to increase the check average at his station and, by so doing, usually increase tips. But a waiter cannot work in a vacuum. Management must establish an effective sales program to aid and motivate the server to actively sell.

Such a program begins with an analysis of the needs and wishes of the market. Restaurant patrons are a captive audience who have decided to spend. Management must see to it that products and services are available that are designed to meet the needs and whims of their guests. In analyzing the market, a considerable amount of trial and error may be involved at first in creating a product and service line. Once the market has been studied and the needs established, there must be ongoing evaluations of the effectiveness of the established line. Communicate with patrons for input on items that could be of interest to them. Actively seek their ideas. Also consider their requests and the frequency of these requests. Find out what the patrons are purchasing elsewhere, and determine if these items

can and should be offered in place of, or in addition to, the existing product and service line. Determine not only what is selling, but also what is not. Whatever products are offered should be moving. If guests are not purchasing available products or services, the operation has lost revenue that some other operation has gained.

Once a marketable product and service line has been established, the next step in building an effective sales program is to evaluate the current sales effectiveness of the whole operation and of each individual member of the staff. The most appealing and attractive products will go unsold if service personnel do not take an active part in selling. In order to sell anything effectively, the seller must have a positive attitude towards the products to be sold. The seller must believe in the product if he is to convince others to buy it.

Sales training is an important ingredient in the orientation and continuing instruction of each member of the sales staff. Daily level meetings and weekly employee meetings which utilize spirited talks, demonstrations, and duplicate work situations are effective in arousing interest in selling techniques. Daily, weekly, and monthly sales charts can also be instrumental in stimulating sales promotions among the staff. These charts will inform management as to who is selling and how much. Monetary or special awards are an excellent stimulus in promoting the sale of any product and motivating the sales staff. Recognition for a job well done is another incentive for excellence.

Management should be aware of the professional service capability, as well as the sales proficiency, of each member of the dining room staff. In assigning work stations for the evening, both of these factors should be considered. If service is carried out by teams, servers should be matched so that members of each team are compatible in their style of service and approach to selling. Management should also be aware of, and on guard against the waiter who is trying to "hustle" the guests — that is, to sell the patron something by overly energetic or underhanded activity. Hustling might be immediately gratifying in the form of extra dollars in business and tips, but the long-term results will be negative; few customers will return. Once the market has been analyzed and the sales effectiveness of the staff examined, management should develop techniques and tools for an effective sales program. (For a review of these techniques, see Chapter 8 — *Merchandising in the Dining Room.*)

The average day of a restaurant worker generally consists of a series of busy and slack periods. While no one wants to work at a furious pace for prolonged periods of time, slack periods represent lost revenues for the operator and server alike. Business can be developed during these slow intervals by aligning the menu to the needs of the prospective clients. Special menus and beverage offerings for brunch on Saturdays and Sundays can create traffic during what would normally be a slow business period. Early evening cocktail business can be expanded by initiating happy-hour-type promotions, offering special prices during a set time period. This promotion can be augmented by serving interesting tidbits to nibble with cocktails. Menus can be adapted to meet specific market demands, as when less elaborate meals and faster service are promoted to stimulate pre-theater business.

CONTROLS

For management, increased sales should mean increased profits. But without the proper system of controls, profits diminish regardless of the amount of sales.

The mutable quality of foods and beverages makes them more difficult to control than most commodities. Food spoils or is burned, by-products and leftovers are not effectively utilized, and portion sizes may vary. Alcoholic beverages are easily manipulated, with portion sizes fluctuating, spirits being watered down and blended with less expensive brands, and drinks being served but not charged. All of this means lost revenues for the operator.

A major concern of management and clientele is consistency of the quality and portion size of a product. Restaurant customers do not like surprises. They want to be sure that they will receive consistently good food in quantities to which they are accustomed. If an employee tries to increase his tip by serving larger than normal portions, not only is the restaurant being cheated, but the customer will be disappointed when, upon a return visit, he finds the average portion size smaller than expected. Likewise, if an employee attempts to generate more dollar profit by short-changing the customer in the form of small portions, the end result will be few return customers. Thus, standard portion sizes should be established and maintained by management. The customer gains by being guaranteed a consistent meal, the management profits by being able to control the amount of food used, and the server benefits by having a steady, regular customer base of returning patrons.

Another important factor in controlling sales is the use of manageable cost-accounting procedures. Whenever food or beverage is moved, there should be a corresponding control procedure that will insure accountability. The flow of goods in a restaurant begins with the ordering, receiving, storing, and issuing of raw materials, which are then prepared and served to the guest. All orders should be accounted for by invoices; all goods received should be logged onto some type of daily receiving form; all materials in stock should be catalogued on an inventory; and all items should be issued from the storeroom to the various production areas by the use of requisitions. Food which is ordered from the kitchen for serving in the dining room should be accounted for with dupes of the guest check, or a food-checkers' sheet. Food served to the guest must be recorded on the guest check and then tallied by the cashier on a sales record.

Theoretically, any item which has been purchased by a restaurant should be traceable from the time it was ordered to the time it was consumed. Control systems will vary from one establishment to another. However, the general goal of each system is the same — to guarantee a profit. This profit can be achieved only if certain objectives of the control system are realized:

The control of all items issued to the established departments

The control of waste, pilferage, and theft

The control of cost by providing adequate

accurate, and accessible information on daily, weekly, monthly, and yearly expenditures and sales, to be used for projecting and budgeting

The control of the cash flow by providing accurate cash receipts, so that the guest is neither over nor undercharged; and accurate payable accounts through exact weights, prices, extensions, and totals on individual invoices and monthly statements

Overall control is achieved in a system which meets these objectives, and so itemizes income and expenditures to spotlight areas which need adjustment and/or improvement. Control systems must be established which operate with the greatest possible ease. The simpler the system, the more quickly pertinent information will be made available, and the more accurate that information will be. This will enable management to act precisely and immediately on potential problems.

In the dining room, controls are administered chiefly by use of the duplicate or triplicate check system, a precheck machine, and a cashier's summary sheet. In the triplicate check system, two copies or carbons are automatically made of the guest check as the waiter records the order. The two copies, known as dupes, plus the original, constitute three existing records of the order — hence the term "triplicate" check system. Each copy of the check has a specific purpose: one copy remains with the waiter to be used as a reference during the service of the meal; another copy is presented by the waiter to the kitchen as a record of what food has been ordered; and a third copy is given to the cashier for reference in making out the guest's bill. Under certain circumstances more than three copies may be needed, as when there are several food pick-up areas, such as kitchen, pantry, and dessert stations. Many operations have separate bar bills to record beverage sales. Theoretically, the particulars from the three copies of the guest check can be reconciled against each other. At the end of the meal period all kitchen dupes are analyzed; the total number of each specific menu item issued to the dining room should agree with the corresponding number of dishes served by the waiter and recorded on his copy. This number should also correspond with the number of dishes for which the cashier has collected payment.

The duplicate check system utilizes an original check and a single copy. The copy goes to the kitchen and the original remains at the station to facilitate service and tallying of the final bill. The triplicate system offers more control, but loses its value if no cashier is employed.

On the surface, it appears that the more dupes which are made, the more control there is. But care must be taken not to make the control system too elaborate, or it will slow service by becoming a hindrance. Control systems must be kept workable so that needed information is quickly available. And too, the more complicated the system, the more chance there is of manipulating it.

Too extensive a system may also have a negative effect on workers by conveying a feeling of distrust. If employee theft and pilferage is high, a control system, however elaborate, will not necessarily stop it. Devious minds will find ways to "beat the system." The best control system begins with the proper hiring and screening of each employee. Of course, not all employees hired will be honest, and controls must be established, developed, and followed to minimize the losses. Periodic and irregular spot checks should be made to insure that all employees comply with the prescribed policies. Outside agencies can be engaged to uncover common manipulations of the control system. Some often-used techniques are:

Undercharging: not recording all of the items served to a guest but collecting full payment and pocketing the difference. The service person could also undercharge the guest with hopes of a larger tip.

Mischarging: tabulating items served to one customer on another's check, hoping to collect twice. This can occur in a busy operation with a large turnover.

Not charging: not registering beverage or food on a guest check and giving it to friends who frequent the establishment.

Cash register theft: controlled by permitting as few persons as possible to handle cash, and by providing adequate controls to cover two or more persons working with the same register. Daily cash audits with even minor infractions recorded and reported will discourage theft. This procedure informs employees that there is concern for detail and that their performance is continually being monitored.

Bartenders have many opportunities to cheat the employer. Diluting or bringing spirits in from the outside, selling them to customers, and pocketing the payment is a common practice. This kind of theft is hard to catch, as regular bar inventories will not reveal the deception. A similar technique is to underpour the designated amount of spirits in each drink. In this way the bartender will get a predetermined number of extra drinks from each bottle of spirits. The payment for these extra drinks is then pocketed by the bartender.

Daily opening and closing inventories are an effective way to curtail the theft of food and beverage stock during a meal period. This takes time and energy, and will cost money, but the added expenditure is necessary to maintain a proper control system.

The Precheck Method

Precheck registers are used for recording the sales of food and beverage before the actual order is placed at the bar or kitchen. The machine is similar to a cash register, but without a cash drawer. Each server has a coded key to indicate who made the sale. Guest checks are written in the usual way and inserted into the machine, which will not register otherwise. The classification key for food or beverage is engaged, and then the appropriate dollar amount. This information is imprinted on the check and on a continuous detail tape, which is removed and tallied daily. This tape will detail the total dollar amount of food and beverage sold during the meal period, as well as the totals for each server. Some elaborate machines will have keys for each item that can be ordered. Readings can be taken to show how many orders of each menu item were sold during a given meal period. A receipt issued by the machine is turned in to the bar or kitchen as verification that the order was registered on the precheck machine. No orders can be issued to the dining room without this receipt or the actual imprinted guest check.

This system has a number of advantages over the duplicate and triplicate control systems:

> Controls are established immediately, thereby eliminating the time and opportunity to alter the guest check.
>
> Records, which cannot be changed, document each sale.
>
> More information is immediately made available, such as dollar volume of sales for each meal period and for each server; dollar volume of bar sales and food sales; and the number of orders served for each menu item.

Summary Sheets

Statistical information recorded on the guest checks may be compiled on a form known as the Cashier's Summary Sheet. For each bill paid, the cashier lists the guest check number, table number, number of covers, food subtotal, beverage subtotal, miscellaneous sales like tobacco, sales tax, and the total amount of the check. From this information management is able to keep track of all issued guest checks; to figure the total number of covers served in the meal period and the subtotal and total dollar volume of sales; and to calculate the average sale per cover. This information proves invaluable for analyzing and comparing business with the projected budget for the year.

The Cashier's Summary Sheet can be expanded to include a tally of the individual food items sold. This information may be used to analyze the menu, and to determine the popularity and profitability of each menu item. By multiplying the sale price by the number of orders sold, the total revenue generated for each menu item can be determined and then compared to the total sales. The overall profitability of each menu item can be discovered when the revenue generated is matched with the total food cost of the item.

Each waiter can be required to fill out a less complicated version of the Cashier's Summary Sheet — a form known as an "account slip." This is simply a catalogue of each guest check used during the meal period and the total amount of each bill. An account must be made for all issued guest checks. Unused, soiled, and incorrectly tabulated and voided checks must be turned in with the account slip, and the waiter must offer a sound explanation for any missing checks.

Modern technology has provided restaurateurs with an alternative to the often burdensome and time consuming system of manual summary sheets. Cash registers are now available which can be linked to computers. These machines provide instantaneous printouts of bar, food, miscellaneous, and total sales; the amount of business served by each waiter; the total number of covers served and number served by each waiter; and the average guest check. The computers can be programmed to break the information into almost any time frame — yearly, monthly, weekly, daily, hourly, and by meal periods or shifts. By tabulating the number of orders sold for each menu item, ordering and inventory information can be made available immediately.

While many of these forms and procedures place additional burdens on dining room staff, the adherence to some type of cost-control system is essential if an operation is to remain solvent and profitable. By staying in business, an operation can provide optimum job security for its employees. Thus it is in the interest of the employer and employee alike to follow established cost control procedures conscientiously.

13
MANAGEMENT

The foodservice industry in America nourishes the nation. More than twenty-five percent of the meals eaten in this country are consumed away from the home. This adds up to roughly 150 million meals per day, or 55 billion per year. Approximately 55 percent of these are taken in commercial foodservice establishments, with the rest consumed in institutional facilities such as schools, factories, and hospitals. Consequently, the foodservice facility has become a very important social center in American society — a place where friends meet, new friendships are formed, and business is transacted. It has become a home away from home, where people can socialize, forget their cares, and relax in an environment suited to their specific tastes and needs.

SERVICE DEPENDS ON SERVERS

The workers who prepare and dispense the food, beverage, and hospitality are an important link in the success of an operation. What motivates these individuals to work in an industry where demands are so great?

It is difficult to find in another field so many cases of the great American success story. Even now, one can begin as a busperson and work up to the top. While other professions become increasingly saturated and their channels of advancement more narrow and fixed, the foodservice worker's profession is still a competitive one, affirming the spirit of free enterprise that made our country great. Women have and often still do confront difficulties in their efforts to attain supervisory and executive positions in most fields. Foodservice operations have created exciting opportunities in top-level and middle management for women of direction and fortitude.

Many consumers have a stereotyped picture of the industry, grouping all workers together regardless of the type of establishment in which they work. The public does not always recognize the spread in status within the industry. For example, a server's post in a grand luxe restaurant and a comparable position in a coffee shop would involve extremely different responsibilities, but each worker is called a waiter.

The foodservice industry combines a perishable product and a service. Success requires a delicate balance between supply and demand — a skillful coordination of product and service. This balance can only be achieved by, with, and through the staff. Thus, a premium is placed on the expert management of personnel. Harmonious human relations between employee and management can ensure efficient working relations. Friction will surface especially in the behavior of those employees who are in direct contact with the customer. Working conditions must be satisfactory or the patron cannot be gratified. To accomplish this task, the supervisor must be adept in human relations.

Given the complexities of human interaction and the unpredictable demands of customers, a state of harmony among workers is often difficult to maintain. One complicating factor for the service employee is the presence of so many overseers. Besides their immediate supervisor, dining room personnel must also function under the watchful eye of the general public. Then, the demeanor of the server must be constantly adjusted to meet the needs of each patron. While one party of guests may wish to be served by an involved and spirited waiter, an adjacent party may prefer a server who is detached and disinterested. Restaurants are a hazardous retail business. Even while maintaining a specific location for many years, many organizational changes may occur. Often this results in a change of clientele and the loss of stable, dependable leadership within an operation. The worker lacks guidance as the business struggles for direction.

THE HUMAN FACTOR

Within every foodservice organization there is an evolving system of human interaction, and no magic management formula exists to cope with such a dynamic world. The noted psychologist Dr. Abraham Maslow (1908-1970) categorized human needs and arranged them in order of importance. Others in his field have since modified his theory of personality and motivation, but Maslow's basic assumptions and his definition of human needs are still widely referred to in the mental health field today. An understanding and consideration of these needs can enable management in any industry to motivate its workers more effectively. In foodservice especially, where interpersonal relations are so change-able yet so integral to business success, it is essential for management to be aware of the basic human needs that all personnel — supervisors and staff alike — share.

MASLOW'S HIERARCHY OF NEEDS

There are five levels to Maslow's hierarchy of needs:

Physiological needs
Safety and security
Love or social needs
Esteem
Self-actualization

Maslow perceived man as striving to fulfill the higher needs only after the lower ones were satisfied. As soon as one need is satisfied, another immediately appears in its place.

Physiological Needs

The most basic, most powerful, most obvious of all human needs is that for physical survival — the need for food, liquid, shelter, sex, sleep, and oxygen. To a person who has been deprived of food, the need for love and esteem will be ignored or pushed into the background until hunger has been satisfied.

In organizations where workers' physiological needs have not been met, absenteeism and turnover will be high and productivity will be low. An employee who is assigned a work schedule which leaves little time for adequate rest and sleep will never be able to perform up to par and will soon seek employment elsewhere.

Workers can be more easily motivated to excel at their jobs if the work environment is physically com-fortable. Controllable conditions such as temperature, ventilation, and noise must be maintained at an agree-able level. Satisfactory work space is also essential. If uniforms are furnished for employees, management has a responsibility to issue only clothing which will fit comfortably and provide sufficient warmth as the work-ing conditions dictate.

Safety and Security

Once the physiological needs have been satisfied, the need for safety and security emerges. People must be assured that the physiological needs will continue to be satisfied. This need takes many forms, as in the drive for physical, financial, and psychological security.

Physical security or the need for safety manifests itself on the job whenever there is a real or imagined threat to life or limb. Work conditions must be safe and free from danger. Restaurant work is physical and all efforts must be made by management to minimize hazards.

Financial security can be satisfied by providing monetary compensation for a job well done, with satis-factory pay scales and fringe benefits. An employee needs to know that the business concern for which he works is solvent and is not on the brink of folding. Sound business and management practices will do much to alleviate this concern. A sense of job security can also be conveyed through positive verbal comments concerning a worker's performance.

Psychologists and teachers have observed in children the need for a predictable, orderly world. Children prefer consistency, fairness, and a certain amount of routine. Without these elements they will become anxious and insecure. Freedom within limits rather than total permissiveness is preferred and, in fact, is necessary for the development of well-adjusted children. The same is often true for adults. The insecure person has a compulsive need for order and stability and goes to great lengths to avoid the strange and un-expected. The healthy person also seeks order and stability, but can easily adapt to change.

Employees have a need to know what is expected of them and when. Much of this information should be covered in the job description. Proper training pro-cedures will also reinforce the workers' knowledge of what is expected of them. Supervisors must not be whimsical or arbitrary in dealing with work situations. Rather, they should be fair, unbiased, and impartial.

Love and Social Needs

When the physiological and safety needs have been amply satisfied, the need for love and affection emerges. Love is not to be confused with sex, which can be studied as a purely physiological need. Rather, it can be defined as affection based on acceptance, admiration, benevolence, and common interests. The need for love is expressed, in part, by the desire for a place in one's group, and for affectionate relationships with people in general. Productivity is known to increase in a warm and congenial social atmosphere. The worker must be made to feel that he belongs in his job and is accepted by his fellow workers.

Esteem

Once a person feels comfortably accepted, the drive for esteem will materialize. People need to be respected in their own eyes and in the eyes of others. The thirst for self-esteem will be quenched when a sense of confi-dence, competence, mastery, and achievement has been realized. The need for esteem from others can be seen in the striving for prestige, recognition, status, and reputation.

A person who has an adequate sense of esteem will be more confident and capable on the job, and hence more productive. A manager can help build this con-

fidence by recognizing and showing appreciation for a successful job performance. Commendations can take the form of an award, bonus, raise, simple memo, slap on the back, handshake, or even such verbal comments as "Well done."

Self-Actualization

The need for self-actualization generally arises after the reasonable satisfaction of the esteem and love needs. According to Maslow, the need to grow, develop, and fully utilize one's potential is an important aspect of human motivation.

If we all have this tendency toward self-actualiza-tion, why is it that so few of us, less than one percent, "make it to the top" and realize our full potential? In part, this is because we are blind to our capabilities. The successful manager will be able to tap a person's talents and abilities, and motivate him to aspire to higher levels of performance.

Maslow recognized that while the human species is growth-oriented, it simultaneously and paradoxically has a tendency towards inertia. This tendency to remain at rest will dominate unless the individual is stimulated by some external force. Healthy people prefer work to idleness, but most people will choose no work over meaningless, worthless, or wasted work. There must be some element of challenge to our activities. A successful manager will recognize this fact and provide the stimu-lation and excitement needed to motivate workers to compete, achieve, and excel.

CONCLUSION

For a business to be successful, healthy managers are as important as healthy workers. The psychologically healthy manager will be able to increase the production of his workers, and will contribute to their psychological well-being as well. To be an effective leader, one must first become an effective individual. Being aware of one's personal needs is a prerequisite to satisfying the needs of those supervised.

This brings us to the concept of power. Many people assume that power in the form of strong leader-ship is always bad, overlooking the fact that there are healthy leaders whose motives are for the good of their organization and of society. It is incorrect to assume that all leadership is an unhealthy hunger for selfish power. The key words are "healthy" and "unhealthy."

Good or bad leadership depends to a large degree on whether or not the leader is psychologically sound.

Another important aspect of leadership is that a given leader should not let himself become too sensitive to the feelings of his followers. According to Maslow, the person who must be loved by everyone is not likely to make a good leader. There are times when the leader must say no, be tough, strong, and courageous. The leader with high self-esteem will have the courage to withstand expedient demands that might be damaging to the organization in the long run. An excellent leader is the one who takes pleasure in seeing his workers grow and self-actualize.

Finally, professional dining room management must be flexible and decisive, making quick and effective decisions. This is an integral part of the product and services that guests pay for and expect. By effectively directing its personnel, management will optimize the satisfaction of its guests and the flow of returning patrons. Sound management practices add polish and professionalism to the establishment, and to the food-service industry as a whole.

APPENDIX

STANDARD TABLE AND TABLECLOTH SIZES IN INCHES

TABLE SIZES	TABLECLOTH SIZES
30 x 26 30 x 30 30 ROUND	42 x 42 MIN. 54 x 54 MAX.
36 x 36 36 ROUND	48 x 48 MIN. 60 x 60 MAX.
42 x 42 42 ROUND	52 x 52 MIN. 64 x 64 MAX.
44 x 44	56 x 56 MIN. 66 x 66 MAX.
48 ROUND	60 x 60 MIN. 66 x 66 MAX.
54 ROUND	66 x 66 MIN. 72 x 72 MAX.
60 ROUND	72 x 72 MIN. 76 x 76 MAX.
66 ROUND	78 x 78 MIN. 84 x 84 MAX.
72 ROUND	84 x 84 MIN. 90 x 90 MAX.
72 x 30	90 x 54 MIN. 96 x 54 MAX.
72 x 36	114 x 54 MIN. 120 x 54 MAX.
96 x 30	90 x 60 MIN. 96 x 60 MAX.
96 x 36	114 x 60 MIN. 120 x 60 MAX.

Table I. Standard Table and Table Cloth Sizes in Inches.

METRIC STANDARDS OF FILL FOR DISTILLED SPIRITS

METRIC SIZES	FLUID OZ. IN METRIC SIZES	CORRESPONDING U.S. SIZES	FLUID OZ. IN U.S. SIZES
50 ml	1.7 oz.	Miniature	1.6 oz.
200 ml	6.8 oz.	1/2 Pint	8 oz.
500 ml	16.9 oz.	1 Pint	16 oz.
750 ml	25.4 oz.	4/5 Quart	25.6 oz.
1 liter	33.8 oz.	1 Quart	32 oz.
1.75 liter	59.2 oz.	1/2 Gallon	64 oz.

Table II. Metric Standards of Fill for Distilled Spirits.

METRIC STANDARDS OF FILL FOR WINE

METRIC SIZES	FLUID OZ. IN METRIC SIZES	CORRESPONDING U.S. SIZES	FLUID OZ. IN U.S. SIZES
100 ml	3.4	Miniature	2, 3 or 4
187 ml	6.3	2/5 Pint	6.4
375 ml	12.7	4/5 Pint	12.8
750 ml	25.4	4/5 Quart	25.6
1 Liter	33.8	1 Quart	32.0
1.5 Liter	50.7	2/5 Gallon	51.2
3 Liter	101	4/5 Gallon	102.4

Table III. Metric Standards of Fill for Wine.

163

GLOSSARY

Agneau (Fr) Lamb.

A la Carte (Fr) Of (or on) the card. On a menu, to price each item individually.

A la maitre d'hotel (Fr) Literally, in the style of the master of the hotel. Generally, a food item that features a type of compound butter made with chopped parsley and lemon juice.

A l'Anglaise (Fr) English style. Standard breading procedure for fried foods, wherein food is dredged in flour, dipped in egg wash, and coated with bread crumbs.

A la serviette (Fr) Food served in a decoratively folded napkin.

Almandine (Fr) Food items prepared or garnished with almonds, as in green beans almandine.

Ambience Pervading interior atmosphere. Result of carefully planned effects.

Annealing In the making of glassware, the shaping the glass at high temperatures and allowing it to cool.

Appellation d'origine controlee (Fr) 1. For wine, French government designation. Guarantees the wine in the bottle was produced in the viticultural area stated on the label; also guarantees the wine was made using traditional methods. 2. The legal authorization for the name of a vineyard or wine region.

Aperitif wine Wine drunk before the meal to stimulate the appetite. Possesses a high alcoholic content and strong flavor.

Apprentice Person learning an art or trade by practical experience.

Aspic 1. A mold. 2. An arrangement of cold food molded in jelly. 3. Cooked slices of chicken, meat, fish, vegetables, fruits, etc. put into a mold lined with jelly. Also, the actual jelly.

Au gratin (Fr) 1. Food item browned lightly under a broiler or salamander. 2. Food item sprinkled with bread crumbs and cheese, then browned, creating a golden crust on top.

Au jus (Fr) Food item served with its natural cooking juices.

Au lait (Fr) Food item served with milk.

Au natural (Fr) Food item cooked and served plain. Boiled foods.

Bisque Thick soup made with cream and a puree of the main ingredient, most often of shellfish.

Boeuf (Fr) Beef.

Bouillon Clear soup or broth, at times served to guests before cocktails in order to coat the stomach and thus lighten the effects of any alcohol consumed.

Bouquet Scent of a mature wine, as distinguished from aroma, which is the scent given off by a young wine.

Bourgeois (Fr) In the style of the middle class.

Breathing See *oxidation*.

Brochette (Fr) Small spit or skewer. See *en brochette*.

Buffet Display of hot and cold foods which facilitates the serving of large groups.

Busperson Restaurant person responsible for clearing dishes from the table and returning them to the warewashing area. Equivalent to Commis Debarrasseur in French service.

Cafe (Fr) Coffee.

Cafe diable set Set of tableside cooking utensils used for the preparation of cafe diable. Consists of heating unit, round-bottomed copper pot, and stand.

Canape (Fr) Appetizer served on a base of bread, toast, or crackers.

Canard (Fr) Duck.

Cannelon Hollow pasta or rolled crepe stuffed with meat or cheese and served hot with tomato sauce.

Captain Person in charge of a particular dining room station and its waiters. Corresponds to the Chef de Rang in French service.

Carafe Glass container with a flared lip, used to hold liquids, most notably wine.

Carre d'agneau (Fr) Rack of lamb.

Chafing dish Holloware used to keep food warm. Consists of waterbath, pan or tray, heating unit, and stand.

Champignons (Fr) Mushrooms.

Chateau (Fr) Castle; fortress.

Chateaubriand (Fr) Center and thickest cut of beef tenderloin.

Chef de Rang (Fr) Person in charge of tableside cooking, plating food in the dining room, and supervising a particular section. Equivalent to the captain in American service.

Chef de Salle (Fr) Person in charge of running the dining room and supervising its staff. Equivalent to the head waiter in American service.

Commis (Fr) Apprentice.

Commis Chef de Suite (Fr) Apprentice back waiter.

Commis Debarrasseur (Fr) Apprentice front waiter; person responsible for clearing the table. Equivalent to busperson in American service.

Commis de Rang (Fr) Person responsible for the proper maintenance of the table at all times during the service. Equivalent to front waiter in American service.

Condiment Seasoning such as mustard, catsup, and steak sauce. Used to enhance the flavor of food.

Connaisseur (Fr) An expert; one who has knowledge of and may appreciate fine food, wine, and service. Equivalent to English connoisseur.

Consomme Clarified stock served with garnish that denotes its name. Fortified with meat, vegetables, and egg whites (used in the clarification process).

Cordial Alcoholic beverage flavored with aromatics and usually sweetened; served before the meal.

Couvert (Fr) Cover.

Cover 1. Customer; guest. 2. Actual table setting used for a particular service, such as American, French, or Russian.

Cruet Small glass bottle for holding liquid condiments, such as vinegar and oil.

Decanter Glass or crystal container into which older, more delicate wines are poured to remove their sediments.

Denominazione di origine semplice (Ital) For wine, Italian label designation. Used for ordinary wines produced in Italy's traditional wine regions.

Denominazione di origine controllata (Ital) For wine, Italian label designation meaning controlled. Usually abbreviated D.O.C. Used for quality wines originating from delimited wine regions, produced from approved grape varieties, and made by traditional practices. Vineyards producing D.O.C. wines are listed in an official register.

Denominazione di origine controllata e garantita (Ital) For wine, Italian designation meaning controlled and guaranteed. Used for wines of the highest quality and price. Label bears a government seal stating that the wines have conformed to certain standards.

Dessert wine Sweet wine taken after the meal as the dessert itself, with pastry or fruit.

Deuce Table for two persons.

Drugstore 1. Area in which condiments are stored, discreetly located in the dining room. 2. In the dining room, a shelf or a sidestand.

En brochette (Fr) Food item, such as meat, poultry, or seafood, broiled and served on a skewer.

En papillote (Fr) Literally, in paper. Food item wrapped, cooked, and presented in the dining room in paper.

Electrolytic reaction An electromagnetic reaction that occurs when aluminum is placed in a waterbath with silver. Removes tarnish from silverware and silver serving pieces.

Estate Bottled   For wine, label designation indicating that wine was bottled on the site where it was grown.

Farci   (Fr) Stuffed.
Fillet (filet)   Boneless tender portion of meat, poultry, or fish.
Fines herbes   (Fr) Mixture of finely chopped fresh herbs, such as parsley, chervil, and marjoram.
Finger bowl   Dish of warm water, usually with a lemon slice in it, placed on the table prior to a course that is eaten with the fingers, such as artichokes.
Flatware   Collectively, all knives, forks, spoons, and serving utensils used in the dining room.
Flax   Plant that produces a fiber of very fine quality used in the manufacture of Irish linen.
Fondue   (Fr) 1. Preparation of melted cheese, usually flavored with wine or kirsch and eaten with bite-sized pieces of bread. 2. Dish that consists of small pieces of food dipped into a hot liquid, such as oil, chocolate, or cheese.
Fromage   (Fr) Cheese.

Garniture   Embellishment of a dish, meant to complement its basic flavor. Normally placed on top or around the item. May be named for the inventor or for a city or town.
Generics   For wine, the broad regions in which the grapes are grown, such as Chablis and Burgundy.
Glaze   Transparent coating applied to ceramicware. Produces a nonporous and lustrous sheen.
Grand Cru   (Fr) For wine, good growth. The lowest classification; used for wines from the Bordeaux area.
Gueridon   Wheeled cart from which food is served in the dining room. May include a heating unit.

Hatelet (hatellette)   (Fr) Small skewer with an ornamental top.
Head waiter   Person supervising the dining room staff in all aspects of service. Corresponds to Chef de Salle in French service.
Hem   Edge of the tablecloth or skirt.
Holloware   Technically, those service items of significant depth or volume. More generally, large service items including platters, trays, and stands.
Hors d'oeuvre   (Fr) Light, delicate tidbit served prior to a meal or as an addition to the menu. May be either hot or cold.

Intermezzo   Course during the meal meant to cleanse the palate. Most often, an unsweetened ice served between the meat and fish courses.

Kosher   Foods prepared in accordance with the Jewish laws. Also, specific foods prescribed as Kosher by the Jewish dietary laws.

Liaison   In cooking, a mixture of egg yolks and heavy cream in a set ratio, used to thicken or finish a sauce. Must be added at a temperature below 170°F (80°C), since the proteins will curdle at a higher temperature.
Lignappe   Little extras, such as mints or petit fours, given with the check.
Linen   Generic term applied to all fabrics used at the table.
Liqueurs   Sweet alcoholic beverages flavored with fruit, herbs, and aromatics. Generally served at the end of the meal.

Magnum   Equivalent of two wine bottles.
Maitre d'Hotel   (Fr) Master of the hotel. Corresponds to the food and beverage director in the American line of authority.
Matelotes   Fish stew made with white or red wine.
Menu   (Fr) Literally, small list. In restaurants service, refers to both the selections offered and the actual printed list of food items.
Mise en Bouteille   (Fr) Put in the bottle; bottled. Wine label designation, normally followed by place name.
Mise en bouteille au domain   (Fr) Put in the bottle on (the) estate. Wine label designation indicating place of bottling.
Mise en Bouteille au Chateau   (Fr) Same as *mise en bouteille au domain*, but with reference to a castle or vineyard as place of bottling.
Mise en place   (Fr) Literally, In its place. In restaurant service, all food and equipment necessary to perform a specific operation in either the kitchen or dining room.

Navarin   1. White stew of lamb or mutton made with vegetables and/or potatoes. 2. Ragout of mutton.

Oeuf   (Fr) Egg.
Oxidation   For wine, the interplay of the wine with air once the bottle has been opened. Also called breathing. Results in revitalization of the wine, loss of acidity, and refinement of flavor.

Papillote   (Fr) Paper. See *en papillote.*

Place setting   Complete set of flatware, china, and glassware in its proper place for service or before each client's seat.

Poaching   To simmer gently in liquid. Amount of liquid depends on the food to be poached.

Porcelain   Nonporous, translucent, fine-grained earthenware that produces a ring when tapped. The two major types are hard paste or Chinese porcelain, and soft paste or French porcelain.

Premier Cru   (Fr) For wine, the first or finest growth.

Proper rotation   Taking food orders in a consistent, established sequence; ensures that each patron receives the correct dish.

Proprietary   For wine, a brand name adopted by the bottler for sales purposes. Has no bearing on the quality or taste of the wine.

Ragout   (Fr) White or brown stew of meat, poultry, or fish cut in pieces of regular shape and size. May include vegetables and potatoes.

Ramekin   (Fr) 1. Small individual baking dish, usually earthenware. 2. Small pastries or tartlets prepared from cheese and pastry.

Rechaud   (Fr) Heating unit designed to be used on a gueridon for tableside cookery.

Retainer   Servant; employee.

Runner   In feudal times, the long narrow strip of linen laid along the edge of the table and used by the guests to wipe their fingers and mouths.

Sabayon   Sweet dessert of egg yolks, sugar, vanilla, and wine beaten together and cooked over a rechaud. Usually served in a glass.

Sabayon set   Utensils used to prepare the sabayon dessert in the dining room. Consists of a decorative pan, a stand, and a heating element.

Saccharomyces   Strain of yeast cells used in the production of wine.

Sakazuki   Small porcelain cup used to serve sake or rice wine.

Sake   Brewed rice wine with an alcoholic content of 17 percent.

Sans melange   (Fr) Without mixing. In table service, refers to the cheese and fruit courses which in Europe are served separately, but which in the United States are served together.

Sec   (Fr) For wine, dry.

Sediment   Remnants that form as filaments in the bottle of robust, red wines during the aging process. Always decanted before the wine is drunk. See *decanter.*

Serviceware   All china, flatware, and glassware used for a particular service.

Serviette   (Fr) Napkin. See *a la serviette.*

Side stand   Small cabinet discreetly located in the dining room, used to store condiments, silverware, napkins, or other serviceware.

Silicon dioxide   Type of sand, used in the manufacture of glassware.

Sommelier   (Fr) In French service, person responsible for the selection, proper maintenance, and service of wine. Equivalent to the wine steward in American service.

Souffle   From the French *souffler,* to puff up. Pureed ingredients bound with egg yolks, with beaten egg whites folded in for volume, poured into a special ceramic dish and baked until light and puffy in texture.

Sous cloche   (Fr) Under a bell. To serve food under a bell, usually of glass or silver.

Spirit   Generic term denoting the alcoholic distillate of fruits or grains.

Station   Subdivision of the dining room with a set number of tables and service personnel assigned to it.

Sterno   Alcohol in a jellied form used as fuel on a gueridon or rechaud.

Superior cru   (Fr) For wine, French classification indicating that the wine is above average in quality, although not as good as premier cru.

Table d'hote   (Fr) From the table of the host. In modern context, a menu in which the price of a complete meal changes according to the entree selected.

Tafelwein   (Germ) Table wine. German wine label designation. Used for the simplest quality category.

Tannin   Acid found in the wood of oak casks, used for aging red wines. Essential to the proper aging of wine.

Tasse   (Fr) Cup. In restaurants, used as demi-tasse or half-cup.

Terra-cotta   Glazed or unglazed fired clay used for statuettes or dishes.

Tip   Originally, an anagram: to insure promptness. Now, a colloquial synonym for gratuity.

Tipping procedure   Criteria used to determine appropriate gratuities. May be set by management, local custom, or tradition.

Tokkuri   Japanese bottle from which sake is poured.

Touaille (Fr) In medieval times, a rolled towel fixed to the wall and used by several diners as a napkin.

Trancheur (Fr) Person who carves roasts and poultry at tableside.

Trolley Ornate dining room cart used to display food and expedite service.

Tureen Large attractively designed piece of holloware, used primarily to hold soup during service.

Underliner 1. A doily. 2. A plate placed underneath any cup or bowl, used for service in the dining room.

Varietal (Fr) For wine, label designation made according to the grape variety from which wine was made, as opposed to region or district.

Villa (Ital) 1. Italian castle or large house. 2. Place of bottling for Italian wines.

Vintage 1. For wine, the year in which the wine was produced. 2. The act of gathering and pressing the grapes. 3. A superior year for the production of a specific wine.

Vitrified Stoneware that has been exposed to extremely high temperatures to create a nonporous finish.

Voiture (Fr) Heated dining room cart from which hot entrees, such as roasts or legs of lamb, are served.

Vol-au-vent (Fr) Round of baked puff pastry, in the form of a cup. May be filled with various kinds of mixtures bound with brown or white sauce.

V.D.Q.S. (Fr) For wine, abbreviation for label designation vins delimites de qualite superior or delimited wines of superior quality. For wine, an intermediate classification, better than *ordinaire* (ordinary), but not up to the standard of appellation controlee.

Wine steward Person responsible for the selection, proper maintenance, and service of wine. Equivalent to the Sommelier in French service.

Zabaglione (Ital) See *sabayon*.

BIBLIOGRAPHY

A

ALKIN, Brenton R. *The Waiter/Waitress Manual.* New York: McGraw-Hill, Gregg Division, 1976.

AURIERES, Albert, and Antonietti, Armand. *Le Service du Restaurant, des Etages, du Salon de The et, du Bar.* Paris: Flammarion, 1948.

AXLER, Bruce H. *Increasing Lodging Revenues and Restaurant Checks.* Indianapolis: ITT Educational Pub., 1974.

———. *Kitchen Sanitation and Food Hygiene.* Indianapolis: ITT Educational Pub., 1974.

———. *Showmanship in the Dining Room.* Indianapolis: ITT Educational Pub., 1974.

———. *Tableservice Techniques.* Indianapolis: ITT Educational Pub., 1974.

B

BEARD, James, et al. *The Cook's Catalogue.* New York: Harper & Row, 1975.

BEETON, Isabella. *Mrs. Beeton's English Cookery.* New York: Crown, 1948.

BEMELMANS, Ludwig. *Hotel Bemelmans.* New York: Viking Press, 1946.

BERGMANN, John F. *Tips for You: 31 Ways to Please Your Customers and Increase Your Earning Power.* Boston: CBI, 1980.

BOAS, Maxwell, and Chain, S. *Big Mac.* New York: Dutton, 1976.

BOLHUIS, John L., and Wolff, Roger K. *The Financial Ingredient in Food Service Management.* Edited by the National Institute for the Food Service Industry. Lexington, Mass.: D.C. Heath & Co., 1976.

BOORSTIN, Daniel J. *The Americans: The Democratic Experience.* New York: Vintage Books, 1974.

BRAUDEL, Fernand. *Capitalism & Material Life.* Translated by Miriam Kochan. 1st. U.S. ed. New York: Harper & Row, 1973.

BRETT, Gerard. *Dinner Is Served: A Study in Manners.* Hamden, Conn.: Archon Books, 1969.

BRILLAT-SAVARIN, Jean Anthelme. Translated by M.F.K. Fisher. *The Physiology of Taste.* New York: Alfred A. Knopf, 1971.

BRODNER, Joseph, Carlson, Howard M., and Marchal, Henry T., eds. *Profitable Food and Beverage Operation.* New York: Ahrens, 1962.

C

CAMPBELL-SMITH, Graham. *Marketing of the Meal: A Fundamental Approach.* London: Univ. of Surrey, 1967.

CARLING, T. E. *The Complete Book of Drink.* New York: Philosophical Library, 1952.

CHASE, Robert M., BME, MBA. "Fire Prevention Planning for Hotels and Restaurants." *Cornell Hotel & Restaurant Administration Quarterly,* February 1968, pp. 89-92.

CARNEUALI, Oreste, with Jean B. Read. *Carving and Boning Like an Expert.* New York: Random House, 1978.

COFFMAN, Charles DeWitt. *The Full House: A Hotel/ Motel Promotional Primer.* Ithaca, N.Y.: Cornell Univ. School of Hotel Administration, 1964.

COLTMAN, Michael M. *Food and Beverage Cost Control.* Englewood Cliffs, N.J.: Prentice-Hall, 1977.

———. *Financial Management for the Hospitality Industry.* Boston: CBI, 1980.

———. *Hospitality Management Accounting.* Boston: CBI, 1980.

CONRAN, Terence. *The Kitchen Book.* New York: Crown, 1977.

CORNELL UNIVERSITY. "Essentials of Good Table Service." *Cornell Hotel & Restaurant Administration Quarterly,* November 1960, pp. 45-60.

CORNELIUS, Ethelwyn G. *Food Service Careers.* Edited by Marion Cronan. Peoria, Ill.: E.A. Bennett Co., 1974.

COTTEN, Leo. *Old Mr. Boston's Deluxe Official Bartender's Guide.* Boston: Mr. Boston Distiller, 1970.

CROCKER, E. C. *Flavor.* New York: McGraw-Hill, 1945.

CUMMINGS, Richard Osburn. *The American and His Food.* New York: Arno Press and New York Times, 1970.

D

DAHMER, Sondra, and Kahl, Kurt. *The Waiter and Waitress Training Manual.* Boston: CBI, 1980.

DITTMER, Paul. *Accounting Practices for Hotels, Motels, and Restaurants.* New York: ITT Educational Services, 1971.

DOI, Madaru. *Japanese One-Pot Cookery, Friendly and Festive.* Tokyo and Palo Alto, Cal.: Kodansha International, 1966.

DUKAS, Peter, and Lundberg, Donald E. *How to Operate a Restaurant.* New York: Ahrens, 1960.

DUMAS, Alexander. *Dictionary of Cuisine.* Edited, abridged and translated by Louis Colman. New York: Simon & Shuster, 1958.

DUROCHER, Joseph F., and Goodman, Raymond J., Jr. *The Essential Tableside Cookery.* Ithaca, N.Y.: Cornell Univ. School of Hotel Administration, 1977.

E

EMBURY, David A. *The Fine Art of Mixing Drinks.* New York: Doubleday, 1958.

ESCOFFIER, Auguste. *The Escoffier Cookbook.* New York: Crown, 1941.

———. *Escoffier — Le Guide Culinaire.* Translated by H.L. Cracknell and R.J. Kaufmann. Boston: CBI, 1980.

ESCHBACH, Charles E. *Foodservice Management.* 3rd ed. Boston: CBI, 1980.

F

FOLSOM, Le Roi A., ed. *The Professional Chef.* 4th rev. ed. Boston: CBI, 1980.

FULLER, John. *Gueridon and Lamp Cookery.* New York: Ahrens, 1964.

FULLER, John, and Currie, A.J., eds. *The Waiter.* London: Barrie & Jenkin, 1965.

G

GINDERS, James. *A Guide to Napkin Folding.* Boston: CBI, 1980.

GOLDMAN, Mary. *Planning and Serving Your Meals.* New York: McGraw-Hill, 1959.

GROSSMAN, Harold J. *Grossman's Guide to Wines, Spirits, and Beers.* New York: Charles Scribner's Sons, 1974.

———. *Practical Bar Management.* New York: Ahrens, 1959.

GUTHRIE, Rufus K. *Food Sanitation.* Westport, Conn.: AVI Publishing Co., 1972.

H

HALE, William Harlan. *The Horizon Cookbook and Illustrated History of Eating Through the Ages.* New York: American Heritage Publishing Co., 1968.

HARRIS, Ellen Adeline. *Professional Restaurant Service.* Toronto: McGraw-Hill, 1966.

HARRIS, Gertrude. *Pots & Pans, Etc.* San Francisco: 101 Productions, 1971.

HARRIS, KERR, FOSTER & CO. *Clubs in Town and Country.* Atlanta: Harris, Kerr, Foster & Co., 1975.

HASZONICS, Joseph J., and Barrett, Stuart. *Wine Merchandising.* New York: Ahrens, 1963.

HUEBENER, Paul O. *Gourmet Table Service, A Professional Guide.* New York: Ahrens, 1968.

I

IRELAND, Richard C. *The Professional Waitress: Training Resource Manual.* Wheaton, Ill.: Illinois Hospitality Institute, 1974.

J

JACOBS, Jay. "Specialities de la Maison." *Gourmet,* June 1979, p. 11.

K

KAHRL, William L. *Modern Food Service Planning.* New York: Chain Store Pub. Corp., 1975.

KALT, Nathan. *Introduction to the Hospitality Industry.* New York: ITT Educational Services, 1971.

KAUFMAN, William Irving. *The Whole World Wine Catalogue.* Harmondsworth, England: Penguin, 1978.

KAZARIAN, Edward A. *Work Analysis for Hotels, Restaurants, and Institutions.* Westport, Conn.: AVI, 1969.

KEISER, James, and Kallio, Elmer. *Controlling and Analyzing Costs in Food Service Operations.* New York: Wiley, 1974.

KOTSCHEUAR, Lendal H. *Management by Menu.* Chicago: NIFI, 1975.

KOTSCHEUAR, Lendal H., and Terrell, Margaret E. *Foodservice Planning: Layout and Equipment.* New York: Wiley, 1961.

KRECK, Lothar A. *Menus: Analysis and Planning.* Edited by Jule Wilkinson. Boston: CBI, 1974.

L

LAVENTHAL, KREKSTEIN, HARWATH AND HORWATH. *Uniform System of Accounts for Restaurants.* 4th rev. ed. Chicago: National Restaurant Association, 1968.

LEARNING RESOURCES CENTER OF THE CULINARY INSTITUTE OF AMERICA. *The Professional Chef's Knife.* Boston: CBI, 1980.

LEHRMAN, Lewis. *Dining Room Service.* New York: ITT Educational Services, 1971.

LILLICRAP, D.R. *Food and Beverage Service.* London: Edward Arnold, 1971.

LONGREE, Karla, PhD. *Quantity Food Sanitation.* New York: Wiley, Interscience, 1972.

LONGREE, Karla, and Blakee, Gertrude G. *Sanitary Techniques in Food Service.* New York: Wiley, 1971.

LUNDBERG, Donald E., and Kotscheuar, Lendal H. *Understanding Cooking.* New York: Wiley, 1970.

M

MAGER, Robert, and Beach, Kenneth M., Jr. *Developing Vocational Instruction.* Palo Alto, Cal.: Fearon, 1967.

MILLER, Jack E. *Cooperative Education Workbook for Foodservice/Hospitality.* Boston: CBI, 1980.

———. *Menu Pricing and Strategy.* Boston: CBI, 1980.

MOK, Charles. *Practical Hors D'Oeuvre and Canape Art.* Boston: CBI, 1980.

———. *Practical Salad and Dessert Art.* Boston: CBI, 1980.

MONTAGNE, Prosper. *The New Larousse Gastronomique.* Translated by Marion Hunter, M.I.L. American editor: Charlotte Turgeon. New York: Crown, 1977.

MORRIS, Helen. *Portrait of a Chef: The Life of Alexis Soyer.* Chicago: Univ. of Chicago Press, 1975.

O

OJAKANGAS, Beatrice A. *The Complete Menu Party Book.* New York: Crown, 1972.

OLIVER, Raymond. *The French at the Table.* Translated by Claude Durrell. London: Wine & Food Society, 1967.

P

PERIKLI, George. *Everything You Always Wanted to Know About Bartending.* New York: Vantage Press, 1972.

POPPER, Kathryn. *Honorable Hibachi.* New York: Simon & Shuster, 1965.

R

RENARD, Georges. *Life and Work in Prehistoric Times.* New York: Barnes & Noble, 1968.

RENSBERGER, BOYCE. "New Debate Seen on Why Man First Walked Erect." *New York Times,* 30 June 1979, C1-2.

RESTAURANT BUSINESS, INC. *Menu Planning and Foods Merchandising.* New York: ITT Educational Service, 1971.

RICHARDSON, Treva M. *Sanitation for Food Service Workers.* Chicago: CBI, 1969.

ROOT, Waverly, and deRochement, Richard. *Eating in America: A History.* New York: William Morrow, 1976.

S

SEABURG, Albin G. *Menu Design, Merchandising and Marketing.* Chicago: Institutions/Volume Feeding Management, 1971.

SER-VO-TEL INSTITUTE. *Cashiering.* Edited by Joanne M. O'Hara. Boston: CBI, 1974.

———. *Customer/Employee Relationship.* Edited by Joanne M. O'Hara. Boston: CBI, 1974.

SOLOMON, Ed. *Service is an Honorable Profession.* Vermilian, Ohio: McGarvey's Boat Drive-In Restaurant, 1971.

SONNENSCHMIDT, Frederic H., and Nicolas, Jean. *The Professional Chef's Art of Garde Manger.*

Edited by Jule Wilkinson. Boston: Institutions/ Volume Feeding, 1973.

SPLAVER, Bernard R. *Successful Catering.* Edited by Jule Wilkinson. Boston: CBI, 1975.

STEIN, Bob. *Marketing in Action for Hotels-Motels-Restaurants.* New York: Ahrens, 1971.

STOKES, Arch. *The Wage and Hour Handbook for Hotels, Restaurants and Institutions.* Boston: CBI, 1978.

STRAUSS, George, and Sayles, Leonard. *Personnel: The Human Problem of Management.* 3rd ed. Englewood Cliff, N.J.: Prentice-Hall, 1972.

T

TOURISM EDUCATIONAL CORPORATION. *A Hospitality Industry Guide for Writing and Using Task Unit Job Description.* Boston: CBI, 1976.

———. *Wine Service Procedures.* New York: CBI, 1974.

U

UNITED STATES DEPARTMENT OF HEALTH, EDUCATION AND WELFARE. *Sanitary Food Service. Instructor's Guide for Training Food Service Personnel.* Cincinatti: U.S. Dept. of HEW, 1969.

W

WASON, Betty. *Cooks, Gluttons, and Gourmets: A History of Cooking.* Garden City, N.Y.: Doubleday, 1962.

WATSON, Lyall, Dr. *The Omnivorous Ape.* New York: Coward, McCann, and Geoghegan, 1971.

WEISS, Edith, and Weiss, Hal. *Catering Handbook.* New York: Ahrens, 1971.

WENZEL, George L., Sr. *Motivation Training Manual.* Boston: CBI, 1970.

WILKINSON, Jule. "The 3 C's of Atmosphere II." Chicago: *Institutions Magazine,* 1969.

X, Y, Z

ZABKA, John R. *Personnel Management and Human Relations.* New York: ITT Educational Services, 1971.

INDEX

Note: references to illustrations are given in italics.

173